D0609503

Bloom's Modern Critical Views

African-American Poets: Volume 1
African-American Poets: Volume 2
Aldous Huxley
Alfred, Lord Tennyson
Alice Munro
Alice Walker
American Women Poets: 1650–1950
Amy Tan
Anton Chekhov
Arthur Miller
Asian-American Writers
August Wilson
The Bible
The Brontës
Carson McCullers
Charles Dickens
Christopher Marlowe
Contemporary Poets
Cormac McCarthy
C.S. Lewis
Dante Alighieri
David Mamet
Derek Walcott
Don DeLillo
Doris Lessing
Edgar Allan Poe
Émile Zola
Emily Dickinson
Ernest Hemingway
Eudora Welty
Eugene O'Neill
F. Scott Fitzgerald
Flannery O'Connor
Franz Kafka
Gabriel García Márquez
Geoffrey Chaucer
George Orwell
G.K. Chesterton
Gwendolyn Brooks
Hans Christian Andersen
Henry David Thoreau
Herman Melville
Hermann Hesse
H.G. Wells
Hispanic-American Writers
Homer
Honoré de Balzac
Jamaica Kincaid
James Joyce
Jane Austen
Jay Wright
J.D. Salinger
Jean-Paul Sartre
John Donne and the Metaphysical Poets
John Irving
John Keats
John Milton
John Steinbeck
José Saramago
Joseph Conrad
J.R.R. Tolkien
Julio Cortázar
Kate Chopin
Kurt Vonnegut
Langston Hughes
Leo Tolstoy
Marcel Proust
Margaret Atwood
Mark Twain
Mary Wollstonecraft Shelley
Maya Angelou
Miguel de Cervantes
Milan Kundera
Nathaniel Hawthorne
Native American Writers
Norman Mailer
Octavio Paz
Oscar Wilde
Paul Auster
Philip Roth
Ralph Ellison
Ralph Waldo Emerson
Ray Bradbury
Richard Wright
Robert Browning
Robert Frost
Robert Hayden
Robert Louis Stevenson
The Romantic Poets
Salman Rushdie
Samuel Beckett
Samuel Taylor Coleridge
Stephen Crane
Stephen King
Sylvia Plath
Tennessee Williams
Thomas Hardy
Thomas Pynchon
Tom Wolfe
Toni Morrison
Tony Kushner
Truman Capote
Walt Whitman
W.E.B. Du Bois
William Blake
William Faulkner
William Gaddis
William Shakespeare: Comedies
William Shakespeare: Histories
William Shakespeare: Romances
William Shakespeare: Tragedies
William Wordsworth
Zora Neale Hurston

Bloom's Modern Critical Views

SAMUEL BECKETT

New Edition

Edited and with an introduction by

Harold Bloom
Sterling Professor of the Humanities
Yale University

Bloom's Modern Critical Views: Samuel Beckett—New Edition

Bloom's Literary Criticism
An imprint of Infobase Publishing
132 West 31st Street
New York NY 10001

Library of Congress Cataloging-in-Publication Data
Samuel Beckett / edited and with an introduction by Harold Bloom. — New ed.
p. cm.—(Bloom's modern critical views)
Includes bibliographical references and index.
ISBN 978-1-60413-883-2
1. Beckett, Samuel, 1906–1989—Criticism and interpretation. I. Bloom, Harold.
PR6003.E282Z7999 2010
848'.91409—dc22
2010024832

Bloom's Literary Criticism books are available at special discounts when purchased in bulk quantities for businesses, associations, institutions, or sales promotions. Please call our Special Sales Department in New York at (212) 967-8800 or (800) 322-8755.

You can find Bloom's Literary Criticism on the World Wide Web at http://www.chelseahouse.com

Contributing editor: Pamela Loos
Cover designed by Takeshi Takahashi
Composition by IBT Global, Troy NY
Cover printed by IBT Global, Troy NY
Book printed and bound by IBT Global, Troy NY
Date printed: October 2010
Printed in the United States of America

10 9 8 7 6 5 4 3 2 1

This book is printed on acid-free paper.

Contents

Editor's Note

The introduction expresses my own nostalgia for the lost exuberance of *Murphy*, while acknowledging that Beckett was the author who did most to revivify an almost dying sublime.

Martin Esslin provides an overview of Beckett's world, identifying him as a heretical post-Cartesian, after which Alan S. Loxterman suggests that Beckett absorbed Joyce's theological uncertainty while challenging his friend and mentor's reinterpretation of narrative authority.

Hersh Zeifman then considers the ambiguous endings that haunt the late dramatic writings, followed by Giuseppina Restivo's analysis of Leopardi's influence on the master-servant opposition in *Endgame*.

Lois Gordon turns to the fragmentary nature and dreamlike language of *Waiting for Godot*. Declan Kiberd then casts *Murphy* as the embodiment of Beckett's ongoing preoccupation with themes of failure and destitution.

Eric P. Levy then sketches the disintegration evident in *Endgame*, after which Enoch Brater listens for the essential silences in Beckett's work. Matthew Davies concludes the volume with a discussion of the relationship between the audience and Beckett's illusive stage creations.

HAROLD BLOOM

Introduction

Jonathan Swift, so much the strongest ironist in the language as to have no rivals, wrote the prose masterpiece of the language in *A Tale of a Tub.* Samuel Beckett, as much the legitimate descendant of Swift as he is of his friend James Joyce, has written the prose masterpieces of the language in this century, sometimes as translations from his own French originals. Such an assertion does not discount the baroque splendors of *Ulysses* and *Finnegans Wake* but prefers to them the purity of *Murphy* and *Watt* and of Beckett's renderings into English of *Malone Dies, The Unnamable*, and *How It Is.* Unlike Swift and Joyce, Beckett is only secondarily an ironist and, despite his brilliance at tragicomedy, is something other than a comic writer. His Cartesian dualism seems to me less fundamental than his profoundly Schopenhauerian vision. Perhaps Swift, had he read and tolerated Schopenhauer, might have turned into Beckett.

A remarkable number of the greatest novelists have found Schopenhauer more than congenial: One thinks of Turgenev, Tolstoy, Zola, Hardy, Conrad, Thomas Mann, even of Proust. As those seven novelists have in common only the activity of writing novels, we may suspect that Schopenhauer's really horrifying system helps a novelist to do his work. This is not to discount the intellectual and spiritual persuasiveness of Schopenhauer. A philosopher who so deeply affected Wagner, Nietzsche, Wittgenstein, and (despite his denials) Freud hardly can be regarded only as a convenient aid to storytellers and storytelling. Nevertheless, Schopenhauer evidently stimulated the arts of fiction, but why? Certain it is that we cannot read *The World as Will and Representation* as a work of fiction. Who could bear it as fiction? Supplementing his book, Schopenhauer characterizes the will to live:

> Here also life presents itself by no means as a gift for enjoyment, but as a task, a drudgery to be performed; and in accordance with this we see, in great and small, universal need, ceaseless cares, constant pressure, endless strife, compulsory activity, with extreme exertion of all the powers of body and mind. . . . All strive, some planning, others acting; the tumult is indescribable. But the ultimate aim of it all, what is it? To sustain ephemeral and tormented individuals through a short span of time in the most fortunate case with endurable want and comparative freedom from pain, which, however, is at once attended with ennui; then the reproduction of this race and its striving. In this evident disproportion between the trouble and the reward, the will to live appears to us from this point of view, if taken objectively, as a fool, or subjectively, as a delusion, seized by which everything living works with the utmost exertion of its strength for something that is of no value. But when we consider it more closely, we shall find here also that it is rather a blind pressure, a tendency entirely without ground or motive.

Hugh Kenner suggests that Beckett reads Descartes as fiction. Beckett's fiction suggests that Beckett reads Schopenhauer as truth. Descartes as a precursor is safely distant; Joyce was much too close, and *Murphy* and even *Watt* are Joycean books. Doubtless, Beckett turned to French in *Molloy* so as to exorcise Joyce, and certainly, from *Malone Dies* on, the prose when translated back into English has ceased to be Joycean. Joyce is to Beckett as Milton was to Wordsworth. *Finnegans Wake*, like *Paradise Lost*, is a triumph demanding study; Beckett's trilogy, like *The Prelude*, internalizes the triumph by way of the compensatory imagination, in which experience and loss become one. Study does little to unriddle Beckett or Wordsworth. The Old Cumberland Beggar, Michael, Margaret of "The Ruined Cottage," these resist analysis as do Molloy, Malone, and the Unnamable. Place my namesake, the sublime Poldy, in *Murphy* and he might fit, though he would explode the book. Place him in *Watt*? It cannot be done, and Poldy (or even Earwicker) in the trilogy would be like Milton (or Satan) perambulating about in *The Prelude*.

The fashion (largely derived from French misreaders of German thought) of denying a fixed, stable ego is a shibboleth of current criticism. But such a denial is precisely like each literary generation's assertion that it truly writes the common language rather than a poetic diction. Both stances define modernism, and modernism is as old as Hellenistic Alexandria. Callimachus is as modernist as Joyce, and Aristarchus, like Hugh Kenner, is an antiquarian modernist or modernist antiquarian. Schopenhauer dismissed the ego as an illusion, life as torment, and the universe as nothing, and he rightly credited these insights to that great modernist, the Buddha. Beckett, too, is as modernist as the Buddha, or as Schopenhauer, who disputes with Hume the position of the best writer among philosophers since Plato. I laugh sometimes in reading Schopenhauer, but the laughter is defensive. Beckett provokes laughter, as Falstaff does, or in the mode of Shakespeare's clowns.

In his early monograph, *Proust*, Beckett cites Schopenhauer's definition of the artistic procedure as "the contemplation of the world independently of the principle of reason." Such more-than-rational contemplation gives Proust those Ruskinian or Paterian privileged moments that are "epiphanies" in Joyce but which Beckett mordantly calls "fetishes" in Proust. Transcendental bursts of radiance necessarily are no part of Beckett's cosmos, which resembles, if anything at all, the Demiurge's creation in ancient Gnosticism. Basilides or Valentinus, Alexandrian heresiarchs, would have recognized instantly the world of the trilogy and of the major plays: *Waiting for Godot*, *Endgame*, *Krapp's Last Tape*. It is the world ruled by the Archons, the *kenoma*, nonplace of emptiness. Beckett's enigmatic spirituality quests, though sporadically, for a void that is a fullness, the abyss or *pleroma* that the Gnostics called both forefather and foremother. Call this a natural rather than a revealed Gnosticism in Beckett's case, but Gnosticism it is nevertheless. Schopenhauer's quietism is at last not Beckett's, which is to say that for Beckett, as for Blake and for the Gnostics, the Creation and the Fall were the same event.

The young Beckett, bitterly reviewing a translation of Rilke into English, memorably rejected Rilke's transcendental self-deceptions, where the poet mistook his own tropes as spiritual evidences:

> Such a turmoil of self-deception and naif discontent gains nothing in dignity from that prime article of the Rilkean faith, which provides for the interchangeability of Rilke and God. . . . He has the fidgets, a disorder which may very well give rise, as it did with Rilke on occasion, to poetry of a high order. But why call the fidgets God, Ego, Orpheus and the rest?

In 1938, the year that *Murphy* was belatedly published, Beckett declared his double impatience with the language of transcendence and with the transcendence of language, while intimating also the imminence of the swerve away from Joyce in the composition of *Watt* (1942–44):

> At first it can only be a matter of somehow finding a method by which we can represent this mocking attitude towards the word, through words. In this dissonance between the means and their use

it will perhaps become possible to feel a whisper of that final music or that silence that underlies All.

With such a program, in my opinion, the latest work of Joyce has nothing whatever to do. There it seems rather to be a matter of an apotheosis of the word. Unless perhaps Ascension to Heaven and Descent to Hell are somehow one and the same.

As a Gnostic imagination, Beckett's way is descent, in what cannot be called a hope to liberate the sparks imprisoned in words. Hope is alien to Beckett's mature fiction, so that we can say its images are Gnostic but not its program, since it lacks all program. A Gnosticism without potential transcendence is the most negative of all possible negative stances and doubtless accounts for the sympathetic reader's sense that every crucial work by Beckett necessarily must be his last. Yet the grand paradox is that lessness never ends in Beckett. "Nothing is got for nothing." That is the later version of Emerson's law of compensation, in the essay "Power" of *The Conduct of Life.* Nothing is got for nothing even in Beckett, this greatest master of nothing. In the progression from *Murphy* through *Watt* and the trilogy onto *How It Is* and the briefer fictions of recent years, there is loss for the reader as well as gain. The same is true of the movement from *Godot, Endgame*, and *Krapp's Last Tape* down to the short plays of Beckett's final phase. A wild humor abandons Beckett or is transformed into a comedy for which we seem not to be ready. Even an uncommon reader can long for those marvelous Pythagoreans Wylie and Neary, who are the delight of *Murphy*, or for the sense of the picturesque that makes a last stand in *Molloy.* Though the mode was Joyce's, the music of Wylie and Neary is Beckett's alone:

> "These are dark sayings," said Wylie.
>
> Neary turned his cup upside down.
>
> "Needle," he said, "as it is with the love of the body, so with the friendship of the mind, the full is only reached by admittance to the most retired places. Here are the pudenda of my psyche."
>
> "Cathleen," cried Wylie.
>
> "But betray me," said Neary, "and you go the way of Hippasos."
>
> "The Adkousmatic, I presume," said Wylie. "His retribution slips my mind."
>
> "Drowned in a puddle," said Neary, "for having divulged the incommensurability of side and diagonal."
>
> "So perish all babblers," said Wylie. . . .
>
> "Do not quibble," said Neary harshly. "You saved my life. Now palliate it."

> "I greatly fear," said Wylie, "that the syndrome known as life is too diffuse to admit of palliation. For every symptom that is eased, another is made worse. The horse leech's daughter is a closed system. Her quantum of wantum cannot vary."
> "Very prettily put," said Neary.

One can be forgiven for missing this, even as one surrenders these easier pleasures for the more difficult pleasures of *How It Is*:

> my life above what I did in my life above a little of everything tried everything then gave up no worse always a hole a ruin always a crust never any good at anything not made for that farrago too complicated crawl about in corners and sleep all I wanted I got it nothing left but go to heaven.

The sublime mode, according to a great theorist Angus Fletcher, has "the direct and serious function of destroying the slavery of pleasure." Beckett is the last survivor of the sequence that includes Proust, Kafka, and Joyce. It seems odd to name Beckett, most astonishing of minimalists, as a representative of the sublime mode, but the isolation and terror of the High Sublime return in the catastrophe creations of Beckett, in that vision Fletcher calls "catastrophe as a gradual grinding down and slowing to a dead stop." A sublime that moves toward silence necessarily relies on a rhetoric of waning lyricism, in which the entire scale of effects is transformed, as John Hollander notes:

> Sentences, phrases, images even, are the veritable arias in the plays and the later fiction. The magnificent rising of the kite at the end of *Murphy* occurs in a guarded but positive surge of ceremonial song, to which he will never return.

Kafka's Hunter Gracchus, who had been glad to live and was glad to die, tells us that "I slipped into my winding sheet like a girl into her marriage dress. I lay and waited. Then came the mishap." The mishap, a moment's error on the part of the death-ship's pilot, moves Gracchus from the heroic world of romance to the world of Kafka and of Beckett, where one is neither alive nor dead. It is Beckett's peculiar triumph that he disputes with Kafka the dark eminence of being the Dante of that world. Only Kafka, or Beckett, could have written the sentence in which Gracchus sums up the dreadfulness of his condition: "The thought of helping me is an illness that has to be cured by taking to one's bed." Murphy might have said that; Malone is beyond saying anything so merely expressionistic. The "beyond" is where Beckett's later fictions and plays reside. Call it the silence, or the abyss, or the reality beyond the pleasure principle, or the metaphysical or spiritual reality of our existence at last exposed, beyond further illusion. Beckett cannot or will not name it, but he has worked through to the art of representing it more persuasively than anyone else.

Endgame

Trying to understand *Endgame*, Theodor W. Adorno attained to a most somber conclusion:

> Consciousness begins to look its own demise in the eye, as if it wanted to survive the demise, as these two want to survive the destruction of their world. Proust, about whom the young Beckett wrote an essay, is said to have attempted to keep protocol on his own struggle with death. . . . *Endgame* carries out this intention like a mandate from a testament.

Hugh Kenner, a very different ideologue than Adorno, was less somber: "The despair in which he traffics is a conviction, not a philosophy." A reader and playgoer who, like myself, enjoys *Endgame* more than any other stage drama of this century may wish to dissent from both Adorno and Kenner. Neither the struggle with death nor the conviction of despair seems to me central in the play. An extraordinary gusto informs *Endgame*, surpassing even Brecht, Pirandello, and Ionesco in that quality. It is a gusto quite indistinguishable from an acute anxiety attack, but anxiety and anxious expectations need not be confused with despair (or hope) or with a struggle against death. *Endgame* contrives to be both biblical and Shakespearean, despite its customary Schopenhauerian and Gnostic assumptions. Anxiety, Freud noted, is the reaction to the danger of object loss, and Hamm fears losing Clov. Or, as Freud ironically also observes, anxiety after all is only a perception—of possibilities of anxiety.

Hamm, a bad chess player, faces his endgame with a compulsive intensity, so that he is formidable though a blunderer. His name necessarily suggests Ham, who saw the nakedness of his father, Noah, and whose son Canaan was cursed into servitude for it. That would make Nagg and Nell into Mr. and Mrs. Noah, which seems not inappropriate but is sufficient without being altogether necessary, as it were. There is enough of a ruined Hamlet in Hamm to work against the story of Noah's flood, and overtly ("our revels now are ended") a touch of a ruined Prospero also. I tend to vote for Beckett's deepest orientations again. Take away from Schopenhauer his aesthetic sublime and from ancient Gnosticism its transcendent if alien god, and you are very close to the cosmos of Beckett's *Endgame.*

As in *Waiting for Godot,* we are back in the *kenoma,* or sensible emptiness, a kind of vast yet dry flood. A bungler in Hamm's own image, doubtless the Demiurge, has created this *kenoma,* written this play, except that Hamm himself may be the Demiurge, the artisan or bad hammer responsible for driving in Clov, Nagg, Nell, and all the other nails (to follow Kenner, but with a Gnostic difference). The drama might be titled *Endgame of the Demiurge* or even *Hamlet's Revenge upon Himself.* Kenner and other exegetes have centered on a single moment in *Hamlet,* where the prince tells Rosencrantz and Guildenstern what they are not capable of knowing, even after they are told:

> HAMLET: Denmark's a prison.
> ROSENCRANTZ: Then is the world one.
> HAMLET: A goodly one, in which there are many confines, wards, and dungeons, Denmark being one o' th' worst.
> ROSENCRANTZ: We think not so, my lord.
> HAMLET: Why then 'tis none to you; for there is nothing either good or bad, but thinking makes it so. To me it is a prison.
> ROSENCRANTZ: Why then your ambition makes it one. 'Tis too narrow for your mind.
> HAMLET: O God, I could be bounded in a nutshell, and count myself a king of infinite space—were it not that I have bad dreams.
> (ll. 243–56)

Hamm's world has become a prison, with a single confine, ward, and dungeon, a nutshell reduced from infinite space by the Demiurge's bad dreams. *Endgame* is hardly Hamm's bad dream, but a Kafkan Hamlet could be Hamm, Nagg an amalgam of the ghost and Claudius, Nell a plausible Gertrude, and poor Clov a ruined Horatio. Contaminate Hamlet with Kafka's "The Hunter Gracchus," and you might get *Endgame.* Schopenhauer's dreadful will to live goes on ravening in Hamm, Clov, Nagg, and Nell, as it must in any dramatic representation, since there can be no mimesis without appetite. Where the will to live is unchecked, there are anxious expectations, and anxiety or Hamm is king, but a king on a board swept nearly bare. Kenner thinks Clov a knight and Hamm's parents pawns, but they seem to me out of the game, or taken already. But that raises the authentic aesthetic puzzle of *Endgame:* Is there another, an opposing side, with a rival king, or is there only Hamm, a perfect solipsist where even Hamlet was an imperfect one?

I do not think that Hamm lacks an opponent, since his solipsism is not perfect, hence his anxiety as to losing Clov. The Demiurge, like every bad actor, finds his opponent in the audience, which comes to be beguiled but stays to criticize. Kafka, with high deliberation, wrote so as to make interpretation impossible, but that only displaces what needs interpretation into the question of Kafka's evasiveness. Beckett does not evade; *Endgame* is his masterpiece, and being so inward it is also his most difficult work, with every allusion endstopped, despite the reverberations. There is no play in *Endgame*; it is all Hamlet's *Mousetrap*, or Hamm's. We have only a play-within-a-play, which gives us the difficulty of asking and answering: What then is the play that contains *Endgame*? If the audience is the opponent, and Hamm is bound to lose the endgame, then the enclosing play is the larger entity that can contain the chess game between Hamm and ourselves. That is not quite the play of the world, yet it remains a larger play than any other dramatist has given us in this century.

Waiting for Godot

Hugh Kenner wisely observes that, in *Waiting for Godot*, bowler hats "are removed for thinking but replaced for speaking." Such accurate observation is truly Beckettian, even as was Lyndon Johnson's reflection that Gerald Ford was the one person in Washington who could not walk and chew gum at the same time. Beckett's tramps, like President Ford, keep to one activity at a time. Entropy is all around them and within them, since they inhabit, they are, that cosmological emptiness the Gnostics named as the *kenoma*.

Of the name *Godot*, Beckett remarked, "and besides, there is a true Godot, a cycling racer named Godot, so you see, the possibilities are rather endless." Actually, Beckett seems to have meant Godet, the director of the Tour de France, but even the mistake is Beckettian and reminds us of a grand precursor text, Alfred Jarry's "The Passion Considered as an Uphill Bicycle Race," with its superb start: "Barabbas, slated to race, was scratched."

Nobody is scratched in *Waiting for Godot*, but nobody gets started either. I take it that "Godot" is an emblem for "recognition," and I thereby accept Deirdre Bair's tentative suggestion that the play was written while Beckett waited for recognition, for his novels to be received and appreciated, within the canon. A man waiting for recognition is more likely than ever to be obsessed that his feet should hurt continually and perhaps to be provoked also to the memory that his own father invariably wore a bowler hat and a black coat.

A play that moves from "Nothing to be done" (referring to a recalcitrant boot) on to "Yes, let's go," after which they do not move, charmingly does not progress at all. Time, the enemy above all others for the Gnostics, is the adversary in *Waiting for Godot*, as it was in Beckett's *Proust*. That would be a minor truism, if the play was not set in the world made not by Plato's Demiurge but by the Demiurge of Valentinus, for whom time is hardly the moving image of eternity:

> When the Demiurge further wanted to imitate also the boundless, eternal, infinite, and timeless nature of the Abyss, but could not express its immutable eternity, being as he was a fruit of defect, he embodied their eternity in times, epochs, and great numbers of years, under the delusion that by the quantity of times he could represent their infinity. Thus truth escaped him and he followed the lie.

Blake's way of saying this was to remind us that in equivocal worlds up and down were equivocal. Estragon's way is: "Who am I to tell my private nightmares to if I can't tell them to you?" Lucky's way is the most Gnostic, since how could the *kenoma* be described any better than this?

> the earth in the great cold the great dark the air and the earth abode of stones in the great cold alas alas in the year of their Lord six hundred and something the air the earth the sea the earth abode of stones in the great deeps the great cold on sea on land and in the air I resume for reasons unknown in spite of the tennis the facts are there but time will tell I resume alas alas on on in short in fine on on abode of stones who can doubt it I resume but not so fast I resume the skull fading fading fading and concurrently simultaneously what is more for reasons unknown.

Description that is also lament—that is the only lyricism possible for the Gnostic, ancient or modern, Valentinus or Schopenhauer, Beckett or Shelley:

> Art thou pale for weariness
> Of climbing heaven and gazing on the earth,
> Wandering companionless
> Among the stars that have a different birth—
> And ever changing, like a joyless eye
> That finds no object worth its constancy?

Shelley's fragment carefully assigns the stars to a different birth, shared with our imaginations, a birth that precedes the Creation-Fall that gave us the cosmos of *Waiting for Godot.* When the moon rises, Estragon contemplates it in a Shelleyan mode: "Pale for weariness . . . of climbing heaven and gazing on the likes of us." This negative epiphany, closing act 1, is answered by another extraordinary Shelleyan allusion, soon after the start of act 2:

VLADIMIR: We have that excuse.
ESTRAGON: It's so we won't hear.
VLADIMIR: We have our reasons.
ESTRAGON: All the dead voices.
VLADIMIR: They make a noise like wings.
ESTRAGON: Like leaves.
VLADIMIR: Like sand.
ESTRAGON: Like leaves.
Silence.
VLADIMIR: They all speak at once.
ESTRAGON: Each one to itself.
Silence.
VLADIMIR: Rather they whisper.
ESTRAGON: They rustle.
VLADIMIR: They murmur.
ESTRAGON: They rustle.
Silence.
VLADIMIR: What do they say?
ESTRAGON: They talk about their lives.
VLADIMIR: To have lived is not enough for them.
ESTRAGON: They have to talk about it.
VLADIMIR: To be dead is not enough for them.
ESTRAGON: It is not sufficient.
Silence.
VLADIMIR: They make a noise like feathers.
ESTRAGON: Like leaves.
VLADIMIR: Like ashes.
ESTRAGON: Like leaves.
Long silence.
VLADIMIR: Say something!

It is the ultimate, dark transumption of Shelley's fiction of the leaves in the apocalyptic "Ode to the West Wind." Involuntary Gnostics, Estragon and Vladimir are beyond apocalypse, beyond any hope for this world. A tree may bud overnight, but this is not so much like an early miracle (as Kenner says) as it is "another of your nightmares" (as Estragon says). The reentry of the blinded Pozzo, now reduced to crying "Help!" is the drama's most poignant moment, even as its most dreadful negation is shouted by blind Pozzo in his fury, after Vladimir asks a temporal question once too often:

> POZZO: (*suddenly furious*). Have you not done tormenting me with your accursed time! It's abominable! When! When! One day, is that not enough for you, one day he went dumb, one day I went blind, one day we'll go deaf, one day we were born, one day we shall die, the same day, the same second, is that not enough for you? (*Calmer.*) They give birth astride of a grave, the light gleams an instant, then it's night once more.

Pozzo, originally enough of a brute to be a Demiurge himself, is now another wanderer in the darkness of the *kenoma.* Estragon's dreadful question, as to whether Pozzo may not have been Godot, is answered negatively by Vladimir but with something less than perfect confidence. Despite the boy's later testimony, I suspect that the tragicomedy centers precisely there: In the possible identity of Godot and Pozzo, in the unhappy intimation that the Demiurge is not only the god of this world, the spirit of Schopenhauer's will to live, but the only god that can be uncovered anywhere, even anywhere out of this world.

MARTIN ESSLIN

Telling It How It Is: Beckett and the Mass Media

Although a Nobel Prize Laureate and modern classic whose plays are performed the world over, Samuel Beckett nevertheless has the reputation of being a difficult and depressing author. Indeed, that is how he strikes many people who see his work performed. And their impressions do accurately reflect their reactions: those people *are* puzzled, mystified, and depressed by his works.

Beckett certainly never set out to entertain or please anyone. He writes strictly for himself—or rather, his work is an attempt to explore himself and the nature of his consciousness, to reach to the inner core of that mysterious entity called his own individual Self.

As a Cartesian, albeit a heretical one, Beckett is convinced that our own individual consciousness is the only aspect, the only segment of the world to which we have direct access, which we can *know*. "Cogito, ergo sum" was Descartes's phrase—"I think, therefore I am"; but Beckett modifies it to "I am conscious, therefore I am," and he adds the questions: Who, then, am I? What is consciousness? and what do we mean by "Being"?

Beckett is a poet, an artist, yes, but above all he is an explorer. His work—his prose narratives, plays, mimes, radio and television plays, and his film—all form part of a vast whole, an exploration of the questions just posed. Thus Beckett starts from zero: we can know nothing of the world except

---

From *The World of Samuel Beckett*, edited by Joseph H. Smith, pp. 204-16. Published by the Johns Hopkins University Press.

through our consciousness. So the individual must start with a completely clean slate, no preconceptions, whether religious, philosophical, scientific, or merely commonsensical—no traditionally accepted truths, only the evidence of his own consciousness.

In one of his rare theoretical pronouncements, not about his own work but about that of certain modern painters, Beckett speaks of the situation of the modern artist in a world where all the religious, philosophical, and political certainties have been swept away in the aftermath of the catastrophe of World War II and the collapse of all previously established systems of belief. A world in which, as he says, the artist has nothing left but "the expression that there is nothing to express, nothing with which to express, nothing from which to express, no power to express, no desire to express, together with the obligation to express" (Beckett 1949, 17). Thus, the obligation to express himself in the face of this total negativity remains for the artist the only positive element, the germ from which a new system of values might perhaps be made to grow. The obligation to express contains an ethical imperative: be truthful, have the courage to face the immense negativity of a universe, the meaning of which, if it does have one, will forever be beyond our reach, forever inaccessible. Truthfulness and courage are thus the cornerstones of a new scale of values for human conduct. Cut out all inessential details, don't lose yourself in the description of accidentals, get down to the bare facts of existence and face them; follow your inner compulsion and obligation to express your experience of the world regardless of any incidental considerations—audience response, financial gain, fame, or personal popularity.

This attitude, of course, is along the same lines as that of the existential philosophers who flourished in Paris in the forties and fifties, led by Camus and Sartre. I doubt whether Beckett was directly influenced by them. His own austere code of conduct would have precluded simply hitching a ride on other thinkers' ideas. No, I firmly believe that he arrived at his existential ontology purely by observing his own consciousness and exploring its problems. Moreover, of all the existentialists, he is the most consistent.

If the existentialist view, starting from Kierkegaard, has always been that any thought can only be the expression of an individual consciousness and that therefore ideas put in a generalized abstract form and claiming universal validity must of necessity be false, the French existentialists of the Paris school contradicted this principle by pontificating in general terms and writing philosophical treatises claiming universal validity. Beckett is an existential thinker who consistently refrains from uttering any generalized thought or universally valid truth. His work is strictly an exploration of his own experience, of his own "being in the world." He has, in a career spreading over some forty years of fame, consistently refused ever to utter a theoretical interpretation or comment on his own work. His work must speak for itself, in all its ambiguity and open-endedness. When asked who Godot was supposed to be, he replied that if he knew who Godot was he would have had to put it into the play, for withholding that information would have been cheating, willful mystification of a paying audience.

In a letter to a friend, the director Alan Schneider, who was about to embark on a production of *Endgame*, Beckett wrote in December 1957:

> When it comes to journalists I feel the only line is to refuse to be involved in exegesis of any kind. And to insist on the extreme simplicity of dramatic situation and issue. If that is not enough for them, and it obviously isn't, it's plenty for us, and we have no elucidation to offer of mysteries that are all of their making. My work is a matter of fundamental sounds (no joke intended) made as fully as possible, and I accept responsibility for nothing else. If people want to have headaches among the overtones, let them. And provide their own aspirin. Hamm as stated, Clov as stated, together as stated, nec tecum nec sine te, in such a place, in such a world, that's all I can manage, more than I could. [1983, 109]

Fundamental sounds—and no joke intended! The work is an emanation of himself, a natural and spontaneous outflow of his consciousness.

I once asked Beckett how he went about his work. He replied that he sat down in front of a blank piece of paper and then waited till he heard the voice within him. He faithfully took down what the voice said—and then, he added, of course, he applied his sense of form to the product. This is very much like the program of the surrealists, led by André Breton (himself a psychoanalyst), who wanted to tap the poetic sources of the unconscious by automatic writing.

Beckett experiences himself, his consciousness, the principal evidence of his "being," as a continuous stream of words. He, and most human beings, thus can be seen to appear to themselves mainly as a narrative, and ongoing story; or perhaps a dialogue, for our consciousness contains contradictory ideas and impulses and thus frequently discussions and debates, fierce struggles between them.

Where, then, Beckett asks himself, is the core, the center, the true essence of my "being," of being in the world as such?

Yet, in trying to observe the nature of his own self, Beckett comes to the recognition of another split in the self. Not only are there often several voices in contention and debate—"Should I smoke? I want to smoke! No, it is bad for my health!"—but the very fact of being conscious, being aware of one's own being as a stream of words, already implies a split: into an observer on the one hand and that which is being observed on the other. There is someone—myself—who listens to the narrative that emanates from myself, and the moment I try to catch the essence of the self that speaks the words I hear in my consciousness, the observer has already become the observed. It is an endless quest: the two halves can never come together, except perhaps at one of those moments of miraculous insight or illumination of which all mystical religions speak—the mystical unity with the absolute, satori—but which seems to be denied to modern secularized Western man.

We experience ourselves and the world through a stream of consciousness, an interior monologue, a continuous murmured narrative. Beckett's work thus is overwhelmingly interior monologue. The few texts that contain descriptions of strange unworldly worlds are clearly accounts of dreams. There is in them no description of objects from the outside—objectively seen. In his early essay on Proust, Beckett expresses contempt for writers who spend their time in describing the outside world, clothes, landscapes, furniture. He feels that doing this is a waste of time, a whistling in the dark, a concentration on the accidentals of human existence rather than its essential nature. Such description is like the listing of items in an inventory, a mindless chore.

For him the art of writing must be more than the mere recitation of externally observed objects. In one of his earliest published writings, an essay he contributed about the work of his revered friend and model James Joyce, Beckett speaks of Joyce's use of language in that strange novel *Finnegans Wake*, in which every sentence contains puns and assonances to a multitude of languages:

> You complain that this stuff is not written in English. It is not written at all. It is not to be read. It is to be looked at and listened to. His writing is not *about* something; *it is that something itself*. . . . When the sense is sleep, the words go to sleep. . . . When the sense is dancing, the words dance. . . . This writing that you find so obscure is a quintessential extraction of language and painting and gesture, with all the inevitable clarity of the old articulation. Here is the savage economy of hieroglyphics. Here words are not the polite contortions of 20th century printer's ink. They are alive. [Beckett 1929, 27; emphasis in original]

Beckett's language is far more austere than that of *Finnegans Wake*. But his work too is not *about* something; it is that something: the direct distillation of a living experience, not a reconstruction of it "recollected in tranquillity." In other words, even Beckett's novels are not narrative but drama: these monologues can be acted without any adaptation—and they have been. The BBC's radio drama department, with which I have been connected for a long time, has broadcast most of Beckett's so-called novels and stories as drama, as dramatic monologues fully realized by actors. And, of course, the need to have the words not only read but listened to, seen as paintings are seen, experienced as gestures are experienced, logically leads to more elaborate forms of drama.

Yes, but drama, immediate as it is, purports to be an objective representation of the world with people in it seen from the outside, does it not?

Not, I submit, in Beckett's dramatic work: here the dialogues between parts of the self, the dreams in which the self debates with itself, are translated into dramatic form.

All drama, it could be argued, is of this nature: the playwright of necessity dreams up the characters and the plot; ultimately it is all an individual's fantasy world that reaches the stage. Think of Pirandello's six characters, who once conceived will not lie down and who demand to be fully realized: they are clearly the creatures of the author's own consciousness, half-objectified and then abandoned. True enough, but most playwrights think they are dealing with an objective world, that they are translating observation of people in that world into drama.

In Beckett's case the characters are far more clearly and openly products of a single consciousness; most of Beckett's plays are strictly monodramas, monologues split up into different voices. There is thus also a clear connection between Beckett's approach and split states of mind. Although Beckett, the sanest of men, is anything but a schizophrenic, he is deeply interested in schizophrenic phenomena: voices in the head, split personalities, compulsive rituals—such as Molloy's compulsion to go through all his sucking stones without ever sucking one of them twice in the same sequence—and, above all, withdrawal symptoms.

Murphy, in Beckett's early novel of that name, is so fascinated by schizophrenics that he takes a job as a male nurse in a lunatic asylum and spends his time observing the catatonic Mr. Endon. In *Endgame* Hamm speaks about a painter he had known who had painted the world in all its vivid colors; yet, one day he stopped painting, and when he went to his window and looked out at the landscape with all the waving yellow corn, he could see nothing but ashes.

One day, while a radio director at the BBC, I was in the studio recording a broadcast of Beckett's *Texts for Nothing*—a series of short prose pieces—when Beckett, who happened to be passing through London, unexpectedly walked in. The late Patrick Magee, one of Beckett's favorite actors, was reading one of these texts with his velvety Irish voice in his usual masterly manner.

Beckett listened with great concentration; and then, with his usual courtesy and kindness, he praised Magee's rendering, but he added: "Don't give it so much emphasis. Remember, this comes from a man who is sitting by a window; he sees the world passing by just a few yards away, but to him all this is hundreds of miles away."

And in the play *Not I* we have just a mouth lit up in the complete darkness of the stage, from which issues an incessant drone of words, a voice that cannot be stopped, a voice that the owner of the mouth does not recognize as being her own, so that each time she is tempted to use the pronoun "I" she screams, "No, she, she, not I." In other words, she is an individual who experiences the words resounding in her head as being someone else's voice, which drones on in her head and issues through her mouth.

Voices in the head, voices incessantly droning on without the subject's control over them, voices that have to be taken down and put on the blank page, these are the basis of Beckett's exploration of his consciousness, the basis of his work. He regards the schizophrenic mind merely as an extreme example of how the human mind in general works. Understandably, though a master of words, a great poet, Beckett is not enamored of the raw material of which these voices are composed: words, language. In the earliest phase of Beckett's fame, a student once asked him about the contradiction between his pessimism about the possibility of genuine communication among human beings, on the one hand, and his being a writer using language, on the other. Beckett is reported to have said: "On n'a que les mots, monsieur"—words, that is all we have!

From the very beginning, Beckett was impatient with language and its use in literature. In an early document, a letter he wrote to Axel Kaun, a German friend, in 1937—which has only relatively recently been published—Beckett said:

> It is indeed becoming more and more difficult, even senseless for me to write an official English. And more and more my own language appears to me like a veil that must be torn apart in order to get at the things (or Nothingness) behind. Grammar and Style. To me they seem to have become as irrelevant as a Victorian bathing suit or the imperturbability of a true gentleman. A Mask. Let us hope the time will come, thank God that in certain circles it has already come, when language is most efficiently used where it is most efficiently misused. As we cannot eliminate language all at once, we should at least leave nothing undone that might contribute to its falling into disrepute. To bore one hole after another in it, until what lurks behind it—be it something or nothing—begins

> to seep through: I cannot imagine a higher goal for a writer today. Or is literature alone to remain behind in the old lazy ways that have been so long ago abandoned by music and painting? Is there something paralyzingly holy in the vicious nature of the word that is not found in the elements of the other arts? Is there any reason why the terrible materiality of the word surface should not be capable of being dissolved, like, for example, the sound surface, torn by enormous pauses of Beethoven's Seventh Symphony. [1983, 171]

Thus Beckett in 1937. His whole career, his progress as a writer, can be seen as an attempt to grapple with this program he set himself more than half a century ago. First his decision after the war to write some of his major works in French—demanding a new discipline, a new economy in the use of a language that was not his mother tongue. And then his gradual veering from long prose pieces toward dramatic forms.

For in drama as a medium of expression the word is no longer the only or even the principal element: in drama the visual elements supplement and undermine the word. The famous ending of the two acts of *Waiting for Godot*—when the words "Let's go" are followed by the stage direction: "They do not move"—illustrates that point. Here a hole is being bored into the surface of the words; the words are being invalidated by action and image. Beckett's dramatic work—and much of his later prose—can be seen as a steady move toward the dominance of the image. The image is not a description of something: it is that something directly, to come back to Beckett's essay about Joyce. In being confronted by an image the spectator is not being given a linear, verbal description or explanation; he is undergoing an "experience." He himself must unravel that experience, make of it what he will, evaluate its impact, which is immediate and both conscious and subliminal and will even directly act on the unconscious levels of his mind. An image, moreover (as advertisers know only too well), lingers in the mind and is more intensely and lastingly remembered simply because it is so concise, because it compresses so many distinct elements into an indivisible package.

Plays like *Waiting for Godot*, *Endgame*, *Krapp's Last Tape*, *Happy Days*, *Not I*, or *Rockaby*, to name only the more obvious ones, do not, as we all know, have a story to tell—a plot to unfold—as conventional drama does. They are essentially images, images that may be built up over a certain span of time. The time it takes to complete the image plays its own part in the final impact of the images: the image of *Waiting for Godot* is only complete when the audience realizes that the second act has the same structure as the first and that the play is, among many other things, an image of the relentless sameness of each day of our lives—waking, living, sleeping, waiting for the end.

Krapp's Last Tape is essentially an image of the Self confronting its former incarnations with incomprehension and wonder as something totally alien to itself—that is the image that remains in the mind, after the details of the words have faded—and the same is true of all of Beckett's dramatic work.

Beckett's dramatic works are thus concretized metaphors, with all the multiple resonances and ambiguities of metaphors as used in lyrical poetry, and they have the same direct impact: they are not about an experience, they *are* the experience. Once perceived, they linger in the mind of the spectator and gradually, as she or he remembers and ponders them, unfold their multiple implications. The great power of such metaphors lies in their conciseness, their economy: in *Happy Days*, for example, the image of Winnie gradually sinking into the earth clearly says something about our gradual approach, with every day that passes, to death and the grave. But there is also in that image the pathetic need for contact with her husband behind the mound, the human striving for contact, however impossible it is to achieve; there is also in it the preoccupation of all of us with our possessions, however ridiculous and trivial, and there is reference to the fading content of our memories in the half-remembered quotations from the classics. These and hundreds of other elements are all compressed into a very short span of time, into a single but multifaceted and rich image.

Beckett is always striving for greater and greater conciseness and compression. He is a man of exquisite manners and politeness—he thinks it is rude to waste people's time with useless chatter about inessentials. He wants to say what he has to say as briefly as possible. Hence also the attraction of the compressed image.

No wonder Beckett's later plays have become progressively shorter and more visual—the role of words in them is being more and more undermined, until, in the end, it ceases altogether. Some of Beckett's later television pieces are purely visual, with a minimum of words, or none at all.

It is from this tension between Beckett's compulsion to use language and his skepticism about language, his weariness of having to listen to the incessant stream of consciousness, that his growing preoccupation with the electronic mass media must be understood. His work for radio, which embraces a number of his most powerful pieces, can be seen as springing directly from this preoccupation. Beckett discovered radio early on when the BBC approached him to write a radio piece. His first attempt at the medium, *All That Fall*, is still fairly realistic: most of it happens inside the consciousness of an old woman, but the outside world with its sounds and the voices of other people is strongly present. But soon Beckett realized that here he had the ideal medium for a stream of consciousness. His next radio play, *Embers*, already takes place altogether within the mind of an old man who cannot stop talking. At one point he remembers how he retreated to the toilet when his logorrhea became too strong, and his little daughter asked what he was doing there talking. "Tell her I am praying," he told his wife.

In later radio pieces Beckett dissects the mind of a writer like himself. In one of them, *Rough for Radio II*, there is a producer, called the animator, and his secretary, who are compelled each day to go down into the cellar and take a little old man called Fox (clearly Vox—the voice) out of the cupboard where he is kept; they have to listen to what he says so that the secretary can take it down. Fox says little of interest, but the animator and the secretary are compelled to do this every day of their lives. They can only faintly hope that one day they will be spared this chore. This quite clearly is an image of the creative process as Beckett himself experiences it.

Beckett's stage work tries to transcend the compulsion of language by the greater and greater use of visual imagery. Deep down, Beckett is a frustrated painter. He certainly prefers the company of painters to that of his fellow writers. His greatest friends have been painters. On the stage the visual image is equally important to—nay *more* important than—the words. The two tramps on either side of the little tree in *Waiting for Godot*, the pathetic figures of the old parents emerging from trash cans in *Endgame*, are infinitely stronger than any words that are spoken in those plays. The same is true of Krapp listening to his former self on an old tape recorder, Winnie sinking into the ground, or the heads of the three dead characters protruding from funerary urns in *Play*, the isolated spot of light on the mouth in *Not I*, the rocking chair with the old woman moving up and down in *Rockaby*. The trouble with stage images, however, is that their realization depends on a director and stage designer who may want to modify the author's vision. The rumpus a few years ago about a production of *Endgame* in Boston, where the director had decided to locate the play in a New York subway station after World War III, is a case in point. Beckett objected so strongly to this modification of his vision (which also completely changes the meaning of the play itself) that he threatened to ban the production; only reluctantly did he allow a compromise by which the theater had to print his stage direction in the program and point out that the set here presented was at variance with the author's intentions.

The solution to the problem of misinterpretation by directors and stage designers lay with Beckett's directing his own stage work—which he did on various occasions, in Germany and with the San Quentin Players. But he could not direct all his work on the stage the world over. This is why he eventually was so greatly attracted to the medium of television. Here he could not only direct his own work but also fix the visual image on the magnetic tape for future generations.

Beckett has always been greatly interested in the cinema: in the thirties he even applied for a place in Eisenstein's film school in Moscow. His plays are full of images and allusions taken from the silent cinema.

In his only foray into writing a film—called *Film*—Beckett chose to cast the main character with that great silent film comic Buster Keaton. It was one of Keaton's last appearances before he died. Alan Schneider, Beckett's friend and favorite American director, directed *Film*, and Beckett came to New York—his only visit to the United States—to be present at the shooting of the picture.

Film, although a fascinating experiment, was not a complete success: the technical difficulties of the film medium, the many technicians involved, inhibited the complete translation of Beckett's vision into the film medium. Taping for television is simpler: it involves fewer technicians and allows the director a far more direct influence on the final image. Although technically he did not sign as the director, Beckett retained complete control of the taping of the works he conceived for television, whether these were produced by the BBC or the Süddeutscher Rundfunk in Stuttgart, with which Beckett had a close relationship.

The short television plays that Beckett had written since the late seventies—*Ghost Trio*, *. . . but the clouds . . .* , *Nacht und Träume*, and *Quad*—fulfill his program of reducing language to the point of zero. In them he has, as in his earlier mime plays, broken the terrible materiality of language and has produced a new kind of poetry—a poetry of moving images that is neither painting, because it moves, nor cinema, because it is extremely austere in the use of cinematic devices such as montage or sophisticated editing.

The short stage plays that appeared during the same period also show the influence of his work with the television medium. Many of them were written for specific occasions, such as the Beckett symposium at Buffalo, for which he wrote *Rockaby*, or the symposium at Ohio State University, for which he wrote *Ohio Impromptu* in 1981, or the matinee at Avignon to honor the imprisoned Czech playwright Václav Havel, to which he contributed *Catastrophe*.

In one case, a stage playlet, *What Where*, has been modified by Beckett under the influence of his having been involved in the production of a television version. In the original stage version, the four men appearing in the play entered and exited rather laboriously; in the television version their faces merely appear out of the darkness. This made Beckett realize that the heavy materiality of entering and leaving the stage was unnecessary to bring these figures on and off, so he revised the stage version to make the faces of the men merely appear out of the dark.

In the play *Not I* Beckett preferred the television version to the original. In the stage version, the audience sees a tiny speck of light denoting a mouth suspended in darkness in the middle of the stage, while on its side a hooded figure—the Auditor—listens to what the Mouth is spouting and occasionally makes a deprecatory gesture. When Beckett agreed to have his favorite actress, Billie Whitelaw, appear in a television version of this play for the BBC, the mouth could only be shown in close-up and the Auditor disappeared. Of course a mouth in close-up is a much more powerful image than a mouth seen at a distance on stage. Here the mouth in close-up became a truly horrifying, menacing organ; with the tongue moving between the teeth, it was downright obscene, a kind of "vulva dentata." I happened to be in the studio in London when Beckett first saw this performance. He was deeply moved by it and, I think, considered it the definitive version of *Not I.* And it is preserved for the future.

Beckett's involvement with the television and radio media shows that he was thoroughly at home in the twentieth century and with its technology. He was a man with an immense interest in mathematics and technology. In working with him on a number of radio productions I was always deeply impressed by his passionate interest in the technologies involved and by his brilliant use of his technical know-how in controlling the production with the utmost precision. As someone deeply conscious of the mystery of time as the basic mode of being, the whole concept of recording sound and images—and thus, in a sense, making time repeatable, stopping it so that one can actually relive past time—fascinated him; hence the play *Krapp's Last Tape* was his direct response to discovering tape recording, when the BBC sent him a tape of his earliest radio play.

His involvement in radio, cinema, and television also underlines another important point: namely, that in our century the art of drama has conquered an immense new field for its own diffusion. Radio and television drama and the cinematic feature film are forms of drama open to all dramatists, and it is significant that some of the most important dramatists of this century have been drawn to the media. Brecht wrote radio plays at a very early stage, and Pinter, Stoppard, Beckett, Bond, and Shepard have written films and television plays. Beckett was one of the pioneers, an acknowledged master dramatist experimenting with the new medium.

It is perhaps a pity that the United States, which lacks a unified television service that can accommodate minority tastes and hence experimentation, is one of the few developed countries where serious dramatists have reduced access to this fascinating and most important medium. All the more commendable are the present efforts of some intrepid pioneers to bring some of Beckett's work to American television audiences.

As I mentioned at the outset, Beckett is still regarded as a difficult author, accessible only to elites. There is some truth to that but only insofar as his work is experimental and therefore does not fit into the stereotyped categories of cliché programming. I have always found it an insult to audiences that ordinary British middle-brow television fare has been thought palatable to American audiences only as "Masterpiece Theatre," accompanied by introductions explaining "difficult" aspects. Beckett does not even fit into this stereotyped category.

But once one has grasped what Beckett is concerned with, he is not difficult or elitist. On the contrary, he deals with the basic problems of human existence on the most down-to-earth level. That is why the prisoners at San Quentin did get the point of *Waiting for Godot*, and some of them decided to devote themselves to the production of Beckett's plays.

In fact, Beckett regarded himself as—and was—basically a comic writer, a humorist, even though his humor is black humor, gallows humor. As one of the characters in *Endgame* says, one of the funniest things in the world is human unhappiness. That is: once you have seen how unimportant the individual human being is in the great scheme of things in this universe, you can laugh about even the saddest aspects of individual experience. In other words: being able to look at oneself and one's misfortunes and sufferings with a sense of humor is a liberating, a cathartic experience.

We can all do with that kind of sense of humor. Beckett's vision is a bleak one; he has none of the consolations of religion and totalitarian ideologies to offer us. Yet what he shows is the need to have compassion, pity, and love for our fellow human beings in this mysterious, impenetrable, and inexplicable universe—and to be able to laugh at ourselves, including our misfortunes. Set against the background of the vastness and infinity of the universe, our misfortunes must appear laughably trivial.

Beckett has the courage to confront the world and to tell us "how it is."

References

Beckett, Samuel. "Three Dialogues" (1949). In *Samuel Beckett: A Collection of Critical Essays*, edited by Martin Esslin. Englewood Cliffs, N.J.: Prentice-Hall, 1965.

———. "Dante . . . Bruno. Vico . . . Joyce" (1929). In *Disjecta: Miscellaneous Writings and a Dramatic Fragment*, edited by Ruby Cohn. London: John Calder, 1983.

ALAN S. LOXTERMAN

"The More Joyce Knew the More He Could" and "More Than I Could": Theology and Fictional Technique in Joyce and Beckett

Through their fictional technique both James Joyce and Samuel Beckett articulate theological uncertainty, the uneasiness of twentieth-century readers about whether reality can be grounded in ultimate authority. In fiction such authority is represented by the godlike narrator who oversees characters and plot and who provides the controlling intelligence from which a normative set of values can be derived, no matter how eccentrically a work's characters might behave or how experimentally they might be presented in terms of narrative technique. The status of this traditionally godlike narrative authority is reinterpreted by Joyce, then challenged by Beckett.

Both Joyce and Beckett question the authority of the traditional omniscient narrator, but do so in ways expressed through opposite stylistic assumptions and techniques. Two examples from *Ulysses* illustrate how the questionable authority of interior monologue is replaced by a secular version of the controlling narrator, the author himself as manipulator of language. Such a narrator is too apt to call our attention to himself and his handiwork to be considered godlike. But, if not omniscient, he is at least omnipresent in terms of style. Two prayer scenes from *Waiting for Godot* and *Happy Days* demonstrate how Beckett seemingly reacts against Joyce's retention of narrative authority, with all its theological implications. Through incomplete or confused dialogue and monologue Beckett dramatizes the difficulty, if not

From *Re: Joyce'n Beckett*, edited by Phyllis Carey and Ed Jewinski, pp. 61–82.

the impossibility, of either the author or his central characters being able to communicate the sort of universal truths that we have come to expect from omniscient narration.

Historically considered, Joyce and Beckett have become two of the most influential writers of our century through their inclusion of problematic interpretation as part of the aesthetic experience, a degree of complexity that requires readers to acknowledge their own complicity in making meaning out of what they perceive. Joyce pioneers the inclusion of indeterminacy in his narrative, first in the opening of *Portrait* and next in those later chapters of *Ulysses* where his method of narration takes precedence over who and what are being narrated. *Finnegans Wake* represents the culmination of a language and style which pre-empts that narrative guidance through a story line which has traditionally been central to the reading experience. Here readers must puzzle over each syllable of the language from beginning to end, being perhaps more consistently aware of their own attempts to interpret what is being said than of anything else.[1]

It is tempting to speculate that Joyce had considerable influence on Beckett since the broad outlines of Beckett's own development appear so similar. First, for both came poetry and an analytical essay on a major literary predecessor, Beckett on Proust and Joyce on Ibsen. Then *More Pricks Than Kicks*, a series of stories set in Dublin and united by a common character instead of a common theme, as in *Dubliners*. Next apprentice work, *Murphy*, which is indebted to Joyce as Joyce's play *Exiles* was to Ibsen. But the more appropriate (and chronologically parallel) comparison for *Murphy* is Joyce's *Portrait* since both seem experimental in terms of their predecessors yet conventionally realistic in comparison to the fiction that follows.[2] Since Beckett wrote many more separate works than Joyce, at this point I shall simplify the comparison by moving directly to some of Beckett's better-known fiction and drama. Like the second half of Joyce's *Ulysses*, Beckett's *Molloy*, *Malone Dies*, *The Unnamable*, and *Waiting for Godot* all represent a departure from the author's previous depiction of reality perceived in terms of plot, character, and setting. Finally, like Joyce's *Finnegans Wake*, Beckett's subsequent plays and later fiction increasingly concentrate on the interior processing of language itself, the interaction between author/narrator(s) and reader which produces fictional alternatives to an indeterminable exterior reality.

In parallel fashion, then, Joyce and Beckett have developed from realistic writers depicting characters in terms of situations into tragi-comedians exposing the provisional nature of what the reader perceives to be their enterprise, truth-telling through fiction. In both we can see the end implicit in their beginning. Even where they retain some conventions of fictional realism, their decentralization of the narrative, through substitution of first-person or interior monologue for omniscient direction, prepares the way for their subsequent shift to an emphasis on meaning as autonomous illusion. Their fiction becomes increasingly self-referential, no longer an interpretation of external reality so much as a construct of language open to multiple interpretations by different readers.

Two examples from the earlier and later types of narrative in *Ulysses* illustrate how the influence of the original Author, as the source of theological omniscience in one's view of reality, has been replaced by interior monologue and by the human author's exercise of his own omniscience through built-in reminders to his readers that he is always in control of his fictional world. When Stephen Dedalus shuts his eyes while walking on the beach, he can still hear the sound of crunching stones and shells, and thus concludes that he cannot ignore the existence of external reality: "There all the time without you: and ever shall be, world without end" (*U* 3.27–28). The double meaning of "without" establishes that reality must be independent of the perceiver as well as external to him, properties constituting possible evidence of an everlasting Creator, as his echo of the conclusion of the "Gloria" in the Book of Common Prayer acknowledges.

Yet Stephen refuses personal assent to that creed by not pronouncing his "Amen." To begin with, there is considerable doubt about how well Stephen is able to read "[s]ignatures of all things" (*U* 3.2). With respect to his own art, at least, the signature is not Stephen's own, but that of Douglas Hyde on the poem Stephen is composing in this chapter (Gifford 44). That night, in Circe's brothel when he is trying to pick out a tune on the piano and is asked by a prostitute to sing (accompanied by the inevitable *double entendre* of having intercourse), Stephen admits that, creatively and procreatively, he is "a most finished artist" (*U* 15.2508).

In aspiring to be an artist, Stephen seeks a kind of immortality. As he would read "signatures of all things" himself, so he wishes to be read rightly, in his essence, by others: "I throw this ended shadow from me, manshape ineluctable, call it back. Endless, would it be mine, form of my form? Who watches me here? Who ever anywhere will read these written words?" (*U* 3.412–15). Considering the literary and traditional associations of one's shadow with the soul, Stephen seems to be wondering here if he has an eternal essence that will continue to be him, "endless" after the death of his human form. If so, can that be expressed in words as a "signature" to be fully understood through all space and time to come ("ever anywhere") by others? The answer to Stephen's question is both someone and no one. Later Leopold Bloom does pick up the scrap of paper on which Stephen has jotted his fragment of a poem. But it has become too blurred for Bloom to read (*U* 13.1244–48).[3]

Stephen's desire to be understood is religious, as well as personal and artistic. At the chapter's end, his original desire to be noticed expands beyond the artist's need for recognition. Wistfully he touches on the Cartesian solution of an omniscient entity bridging the dualistic gap between concept and percept: "Behind. Perhaps there is someone" (*U* 3.502). The name of this chapter is "Proteus," the god identified with the shifting flux of phenomena. So is Stephen looking for the existence of a Cartesian God "behind" that flux capable of unifying internal ideas and the external reality to which they refer? What Stephen sees behind him when he does turn around holds theological promise: "moving through the air high spars of a threemaster, her sails brailed up on the crosstrees, homing, upstream, silently moving, a silent ship" (*U* 3.503–505). The "threemaster" (three crosses, or Christ as the "master" part of the Trinity?) and the echo between "brailed up" and "nailed up" (especially in conjunction with "crosstrees") both provide a possible answer to Stephen's question in an image of Christian afterlife, a funeral ship of crucifixion "homing" toward resurrection.

Yet, as we might expect in a chapter on appearance and reality, this ending remains decidedly ambiguous. For the actuality of the situation undercuts any theological interpretation of what Stephen may see in the ship. He has just placed a piece of snot on a rock, observing "For the rest let look who will" (*U* 3.501). Coming after such a melodramatic gesture, his query about someone behind him may simply indicate Stephen's desire to be caught in the act by some passerby. Or is it guilt over desecrating the rock of Peter's church? In an intrusion rare in the early chapters of *Ulysses*, the narrator inserts "rere regardant," the stiff, even precious, language of striking an heraldic pose, to describe Stephen's turning to look behind him (*U* 3.503). Even the image of the sailing ship may be another example of Stephen's second-hand creativity since it is described in the manner of Tennyson.[4] As a final indignity, this otherworldly, silent vessel's actual cargo is later revealed to be decidedly earthy, politically charged ballast: bricks from England (*U* 10. 1098–99; Gifford 47).

When Haines presses Stephen to describe his religious belief, Stephen responds "You behold in me . . . a horrible example of free thought"; and the narrator notes that he says this not jokingly, as Buck Mulligan would, but "with grim displeasure" (*U* 1.62526). "Proteus" shows that Stephen's misery derives not so much from atheism itself as from Stephen's inability to be a freethinker, to believe in it wholeheartedly as a substitute for the unswerving commitment that he had previously reserved for Catholicism. What begins as comparatively pure internal monologue, a philosophical reflection that reaffirms Cartesian dualism, ends in a yearning for theological reconciliation. Yet such a hope (as Stephen bitterly appreciates better than anyone) contradicts his role of freethinking atheist, which he first revealed publicly when he refused to kneel and pray for his dying mother at her request (*U* 1.207–208). Against the personal melodrama of inner conflict between Stephen's doubt and would-be (or has-been?) faith Joyce overbalances an array of ironic complications. The possible self-mockery of Stephen's viewing the sailing ship in terms of Tennyson's Christian consolation is augmented by the incongruous insertion of the language of heraldry. Perhaps the narrator is insinuating that the reader ought to view Stephen's dramatic "turnaround" toward the heavenly promise of the ship with the same skepticism accorded to his absurd posturing with the snot. At the end of "Proteus" it is impossible to distinguish between the reader's response to the otherworldly appearance of the ship—which, in his earlier works, Joyce might have regarded as an epiphany—and the narrator's own mockery of the notion that any such object could constitute an epiphany.[5]

For the most part, "Proteus" is notable for the difficulties it poses as an example of pure interior monologue uncontaminated (and therefore unshaped) by narrative control.[6] Yet one narrative intrusion, "*rere* regardant," is enough to put the reader in the position of being as uncertain about Stephen's attitude toward God as Stephen himself is. Thus when the narrator subsequently takes complete control, as in "Sirens," the realistic psychological rendering of character through interior monologue becomes problematic.

Leopold Bloom's interior monologue designates him as the main character, among those listening to sentimental songs in the Ormond Bar. Yet Bloom's own sentimental (and voyeuristic) anticipation of his wife's adulterous appointment with Blazes Boylan is overwhelmed by the narrator's larger view of organizing the whole chapter as if its language were subject to the same patterns of sound as the music that is being performed. Consider the chapter's opening: "Bronze by gold heard the hoofirons, steelyringing. Imperthnthn thnthnthn" (*U* 11. 1–2). By the second line the narrator begins treating words abstractly, solely according to their value in creating patterns of sound. Since his epic parallel with the sirens and the situation in the hotel requires that the sound be singing, Joyce adopts the organizational technique of an operatic composer. As a musician might represent his operatic arias abstractly, through instrumental fragments of melody in the overture, so Joyce begins with an abstract sound pattern, the "melody" only, to which the words will be added later. Each of the lines in this excerpt represents some incident that will later be more fully developed as an "aria" set within a narrative sequence. "Bronze by gold" in Joyce's overture later turns out to be a pair of red- and yellow-haired barmaids, the sirens of this chapter who regard a waiter's casual attitude toward them as "impertinent insolence" (*U* 11.99). In the excerpt above, however, we see not their admonishment of the waiter but a typographical representation of the waiter's own sonic parody of their attitude toward him. Closing his nostrils with one hand as he speaks, the waiter snorts out a derisive distortion of "impertinent insolence," an echo (note the number and division of the syllables) "imperthnthn thnthnthn" of the sound included at the opening of this chapter (Blamires 109). Initially Joyce violates our expectations about linear narrative so that we will be more attuned to these fragmentary phrases in the overture when we encounter them again later, as aural motifs repeated within the dramatic context of the narrative.

Of course, the use of words as abstract sounds works against their usual connotations and denotations. The very fact that Joyce's analogy between words and music in "Sirens" repeatedly breaks down is what makes the narrator's arrangement call attention to itself. During the rest of the narrative that follows his verbal overture Joyce introduces rhythmic patterns and words distorted for time and sound values to remind us continually of his narrative concept of comparing words with music, even as we also try to follow the story.[7]

In most of the other chapters after chapter 6 of *Ulysses* ("Hades"), Joyce's narrators arrange chapters according to other abstract concepts. Character and plot are diminished as we become aware, before anything else, of Joyce exposing his artistic manipulations of reality so that readers may see his narrators laboring mightily to create the illusion of significance. Joyce delights in making more out of his subject than it inherently deserves; and he lets us in on his joke. He calls his novel *Ulysses*, the Latin name of Odysseus, to alert the reader that he will be drawing parallels between his own characters and the classical characters of Homer's epic. Such problematic interpretation is also a source of comedy, as we detect these elaborate parodies of well-known works like *The Odyssey* and *Hamlet* and watch for underlying organizational concepts like the one of music just described in "Sirens." Both the parodies and the narrative manipulations operate to distance readers from characters and plot, even as they keep them conscious of the comic presentation, of how hard the narrator must work to invest one rather ordinary Dublin day with epic scope and significance.

Thus far we have seen how in *Ulysses* character and plot are first deemphasized by concentration on interior monologue in "Proteus," then superseded altogether by a conceptually organized narrative in "Sirens." For the reader who surveys the flux of narrative phenomena throughout *Ulysses*, the answer to Stephen's speculation in "Proteus" of who or what lies behind the shifting appearance must be Joyce's narrators and their various organizational strategies. They are perhaps too numerous and various to represent omniscience; yet they do strive to approximate omnipotence by imposing on plot and character a total conceptual order within their individual chapters.

Once we view *Ulysses* in terms of this shift from the microcosm of interior monologue to the macrocosm of exterior narrative control, then *Finnegans Wake* represents a culmination of Joyce's narrative development, a merging of the microcosm with the macrocosm. Through the creation of his own time and space Joyce here invents a language that more closely approximates music than that of "Sirens" because it has become more abstract and self-referential. In *Finnegans Wake* the autonomous narrators of *Ulysses* become one, representing a universal consciousness that is both interior monologue and exterior narration. Godlike, Joyce begins his creation with the *logos* so that his narrator may finally exercise both omniscience and omnipotence, the development of the fiction being the reader's witnessing of a new world being created syllable by syllable.

Like Joyce's Stephen on the beach, some of Samuel Beckett's characters speculate inconclusively about who or what lies "behind" external reality. But Beckett takes the conclusion of Stephen's experiment in introspection, that an external world is "there all the time without you" (*U* 3.27), and shows how this disproves Descartes' *cogito*. Stephen's external world is there "without" him, independent of his being aware of it. Reality is also "without" Stephen in the sense of being outside, external to his perception of it in a spatio-temporal presence that enables him to read its "signatures" (*U* 3.2) as evidence for God's being the prototype of artist as creator. But Beckett's fictions minimize such distinctions between internal and external reality. Consciousness expressed in language through character and narration exists prior to (and so perhaps independent of) physical identity, as a voice without determinate location in time or space. Beckett repeatedly questions the logic of Descartes' "I think; therefore I am" by demonstrating the way introspection discloses no contingent "I" but only the self-questioning consciousness itself (Hesla in Morot-Sir 18–19). In Beckett's fiction, as in Joyce's, loose associative links within the consciousness of narrators replace the more traditional cause-and-effect sequencing of character and plot (Wicker 173). Joyce's novels compensate for loss of such causal coherence through rhetorical strategies that reinstate purposeful control of the narrative. But Beckett's lack coherence; their associative links are minimal because their narrators establish no clear purpose or identity. Whereas Joyce reinstates a full narrative agent, the omnipotent narrator, Beckett progressively moves toward narrative vacuity to demonstrate that there can be no such entity to control the telling; there is only "the weak old voice that tried in vain to make me" (*STFN* 137), the thought process failing to manifest itself convincingly in language.

Throughout a series of novels from *Molloy* to *Malone meurt* (1951) to *L'Innommable* (1953) Beckett successfully undermines both the omniscience of impersonal narrators and the personal identity of narrators of characters.

Sometimes first-person narrators within the same novel even have multiple names, confirming their indeterminacy. *The Unnamable* culminates Beckett's series of minimally narrated novels with an unidentified witness, a protean narrative voice which can be anything from a finite consciousness to an omnipresent metaphysical abstraction. Not only does Beckett's fiction lack the central consciousness of a narrator who knows more than particular characters; it lacks the presence of those characters themselves as multiple consciousnesses who remain sufficiently coherent to reveal discrete points of view on a common subject. For Beckett all conventional narration, from omniscient to first-person, becomes problematic.

In Beckett's first published novel the narrator confidently asserts that "All the puppets in this book whinge sooner or later, except Murphy, who is not a puppet" (*MU* 122). But since it takes a narrator to make such a distinction between puppets and free agents, is not Murphy that narrator's puppet? In fact, who is this narrator who remains bodiless, just a voice that does not (like Joyce's later narrators in *Ulysses*) draw attention to itself as narrator? Does this lack of presence imply that there is another narrator narrating this narrator?

The theological implications of such an infinite narrative regression are most clearly stated in one of the *Stories and Texts for Nothing*. In this work the writer reformulates the prime mover into a prime observer, in terms of Beckett's Cartesian consciousness: "at the end of the billions [of all the peoples of the earth,] you'd need a god, unwitnessed witness of witnesses" (*STFN* 135). But, of course, the work that most extensively dramatizes the impertinence of fallible witnesses trying to imagine an "unwitnessed witness of witnesses" is *Waiting for Godot*. Early in the play, while they wait, Vladimir and Estragon decide to kill time by killing themselves. But they realize this might be impractical because the branch of a nearby tree might not be strong enough to hang both of them, and then one would be left alone—presumably a fate worse than death (12–12[b]). So to pass the time, instead of committing suicide, they begin to reflect on the efficacy of prayer:

VLADIMIR: Well? What do we do?
ESTRAGON: Don't let's do anything. It's safer.
VLADIMIR: Let's wait and see what he says.
ESTRAGON: Who?
VLADIMIR: Godot.
ESTRAGON: Good idea.
VLADIMIR: Let's wait until we know exactly how we stand.
ESTRAGON: On the other hand it might be better to strike the iron before it freezes.

VLADIMIR: I'm curious to hear what he has to offer. Then we'll take it or leave it.
ESTRAGON: What exactly did we ask him for?
VLADIMIR: Were you not there?
ESTRAGON: I can't have been listening.
VLADIMIR: Oh . . . Nothing very definite.
ESTRAGON: A kind of prayer.
VLADIMIR: Precisely.
ESTRAGON: A vague supplication.
VLADIMIR: Exactly.
ESTRAGON: And what did he reply?
VLADIMIR: That he'd see.
ESTRAGON: That he couldn't promise anything.
VLADIMIR: That he'd have to think it over.
ESTRAGON: In the quiet of his home.
VLADIMIR: Consult his family.
ESTRAGON: His friends.
VLADIMIR: His agents.
ESTRAGON: His correspondents.
VLADIMIR: His books.
ESTRAGON: His bank account.
VLADIMIR: Before taking a decision.
ESTRAGON: It's the normal thing.
VLADIMIR: Is it not?
ESTRAGON: I think it is.
VLADIMIR: I think so too [12[b]–13].

The composite image of God that emerges here is so concrete because both Vladimir and Estragon share a concept of what is for them "the normal thing," prayer as a potential material transaction. Godot puts off an immediate answer to their prayer so that he can consult family, friends, and business associates. The progression of consultants grows increasingly impersonal and business-oriented until it results in a personal decision reached impersonally, one based on the proverbial bottom line: "his [account] books" and "his bank account."

But before we blame Godot, their version of God, for being calculating, we should note that Beckett takes pains to remind us that this is *only* their version. At first they are inclined to do nothing because they fear what Godot might do: "it's safer." The scene that shows the tramps getting their first glimpse of other people suggests why they fear Godot. Pozzo appears with a whip, driving Lucky who is tied to him by a rope, a concrete image of the way they have just been discussing themselves as being "tied to Godot"

(14–14[b]). So it is not surprising that they should mistake Pozzo as being Godot (13[b]–15[b]). When Vladimir and Estragon try to put off Pozzo by not calling him by his own name, Pozzo reminds them that they are "of the same species as Pozzo! Made in God's image!" (15[b]); and later Pozzo admits that he is "perhaps not particularly human," when they reprove him for his cruelty to Lucky (19[b]). So perhaps cruelty is that common denominator that entitles man to claim a resemblance to God. To Vladimir and Estragon God is an authority figure responsible for the "muck" of living (14[b]) and therefore to be regarded with suspicion rather than the awe accorded God in a more traditional role as parental authority.

When Vladimir and Estragon summon their courage to make the first move in prayer, it is with the object of finding out "what [Godot] has to offer." Their responses to the way they have formulated their prayer, "precisely" and "exactly," are ironically inappropriate since the prayer itself is "nothing definite." They deliberately keep it a "vague supplication" since they are feeling out someone they know only by reputation and therefore mistrust, hoping to "hear what he has to offer" without committing themselves prematurely to their end of a business deal.

Vladimir and Estragon are not surprised by Godot's noncommittal response, then, because they get what they ask for. Godot's lawyer and agents seem entirely "normal" because this "vague supplication" is tentative bargaining toward a potential contract, not the implicit communication of traditional prayer which George Herbert summed up as "something understood" (Prayer [I], line 14).

Of course, Beckett is suggesting not that Vladimir and Estragon misunderstand the nature of prayer but that they understand the nature of a God who will never answer. If we follow the logic of Descartes' *cogito*, as he himself did not, thinking must be prior to being (Hesla in Morot-Sir 18–19). So there can be no God as "unwitnessed witness of witnesses." Stephen's imperfectly entertained notion of God as creator "behind" the external world may have satisfied Descartes, but it is no longer enough for Beckett. There is only Godot, for only in theory are we made "in God's image," as Pozzo would have it. In practice, as the prayer of Vladimir and Estragon demonstrates, God must be made in man's image, his own language and metaphors based on his own experience.

When Estragon asks Vladimir, "Do you think God sees me?" (49[b]), Vladimir's answer, predictably tentative, comes in an unusually rhetorical passage replete with poetic imagery and allusion:

> Was I sleeping, while the others suffered? Am I sleeping now? Tomorrow, when I wake, or think I do, what shall I say of today?

> . . . Astride of a grave and a difficult birth. Down in the hole, lingeringly, the grave-digger puts on the forceps. We have time to grow old. The air is full of our cries ([*Vladimir*] listens.) But habit is a great deadener. ([*Vladimir* looks . . . at Estragon [dozing].) At me too someone is looking, of me too someone is saying, He is sleeping, he knows nothing, let him sleep on. (*Pause.*) I can't go on! (*Pause.*) What have I said? [58–58[b]]

If it were not for its new context, this striking image of a gravedigger superimposed over an obstetrician might be as suspect as the Christian ship in "Proteus." For Vladimir has borrowed it from the self-conscious orator Pozzo (57[b]), who (complete with atomizer) strikes poses and speaks primarily to hear the sound of his own voice (20[b]). But here the complex emotional resonance of this birth/death soliloquy contrasts movingly with the asperity of the more customary single-line dialogue exchanged between Vladimir and Estragon. Overall, this passage alludes to God's two punishments by which Christians measure their mortality after the Fall: from the "difficult" beginning of birth to the inevitable sentence of death. However painful they may be, our lives seem so short that death appears superimposed upon us from the very moment of our birth. As if to establish that this heritage of suffering after Adam and Eve remains all-encompassing, Vladimir listens for the cries that must constantly be in the air everywhere; and when he hears none, he concludes not that they are not there, but that he has been tuning them out for too long: "habit is a great deadener." At least he can see one other person, Estragon, who is perhaps suffering less than usual because he is dozing.

Vladimir's response to Estragon's query about whether God sees him has been so evocative and compassionate that Vladimir himself finds it inexplicable: "What have I said?" The prospect that Vladimir too may be asleep raises one of Descartes' fundamental doubts about our senses. Since consciousness precedes everything else, how can we know for sure whether, at any given moment, we are dreaming or not? The issue has already been raised:

> ESTRAGON: I had a dream.
> VLADIMIR: Don't tell me!
> ESTRAGON:NI dreamt that—
> VLADIMIR: DON'T TELL ME!
> ESTRAGON: (Gesture towards the universe.) This one is enough for you? (*Silence.*) [11].

Vladimir seeks to get outside his own consciousness by supposing a "someone" watching him sleep, just as he now watches Estragon. But this raises the prospect of that infinitely regressive series of narrators, God as "unwitnessed witness of witnesses" (*STFN* 135). Estragon's original question about whether God sees him (49[b]) is unanswerable because witnessing is all there is. Vladimir can only posit a "someone" beyond himself in a replication of his own experience.

In *Happy Days* Winnie steadfastly avoids wondering what lies beyond her set of circumstances, perhaps because they are so inexplicable. Being buried alive under the constant glare of the sun, Winnie insists that she is satisfied merely to have Willie be her witness. But the way she states it implies that, like Vladimir and Estragon, she would prefer to be a witness herself, in "the old style" of praying to a God who watches over all.

At the beginning of Act II Winnie's invocation leads us to expect that the "someone" looking on is the One speculated about by Stephen, Vladimir, and Estragon, the One whose presence continues to be evoked by our experience of His absence. But Winnie must also "confess" that "I used to pray" and acknowledges that she has "changed from what [she] was" (50–51). Her peremptory invocation, borrowed from Milton, distinguishes the opening of Act II from that of Act I where Winnie prayed personally in silence and then (unlike Stephen) completed the Anglican "Gloria" with her own "Amen." But now the only eyes watching her are secular, borrowed from an "unforgettable" popular song, which of course she has forgotten. So, while Stephen still longs for a transcendent witness, Winnie has settled for Willie. Like Vladimir and Estragon, Winnie fears loneliness most. The prospect of an unwitnessed monologue is her "wilderness" (50), perhaps madness; and she keeps her revolver closer to hand in Act II, just in case.

In one respect, though, Willie is to Winnie as Godot is to Vladimir and Estragon. Most of the time he can only be posited as a witness, and that makes him a source of great distress. Winnie continues to *feel* like her old self, even though from Willie's point of view she will have changed because the mound has advanced to hide her arms and breasts. She is most likely correct in fearing that Willie will lose interest. For sex, including a "disgusting" photo, was most of what captured his attention in Act I. Now she cannot see him and repeats his name ever more loudly in a parallel series of phrases beginning with "what" ("What arms?" "What breasts?" "What Willie?") (51), which suggests that she fears Willie may be her next appendage to disappear.

But concentration on all these changes makes the play seem more dynamic, in the traditional manner of character and plot development, than it actually is. As in the other prayer scene from *Waiting for Godot* where God's lack of response was "normal," here too a countermotion works to neutralize change so that the overall impression an audience receives continues to be stasis, or at least circularity. No wonder Winnie inquires doubtfully, "May one still speak of time?" The constant glare of light, punctuated only by the bells, suggests that the "old style" cycle of night and day has been superseded. Yet Winnie concludes that "one does" continue to speak of time since that is all one knows; the very term "old style" requires a conceptual distinction between past and present to be intelligible. Amidst so much suffering and uncertainty, what seems to be a fundamental change in time could be illusory too. So why not retain the more comfortable older illusion rather than multiply the unknown by accepting a different order of reality? Winnie herself best sums up the effect of her temporal paradox: "Then . . . now . . . what difficulties here, for the mind. (*Pause.*) To have been always what I am—and so changed from what I was" (50–51).

As with people, so it is with events: the more they change, the more they remain the same. Everything—the necessity of talking, Winnie's fear of talking to herself, her need to be overheard by Willie, even the "hail holy light" of her prayer—has already been mentioned in the first act. The repetitive nature of the material, the frequency of pauses designated between Winnie's phrases and sentences, and some remarks in Act I, such as "To sing too soon is a great mistake" and "Do not overdo the bag" (32), all indicate that Winnie's primary objective is time management (to speak in the old style). She must conserve her limited amount of material and pace herself in such a way as to get through each interval between the bells for waking and sleeping. Her smile—flashing on, then off—is as consciously controlled as the bells themselves; and the directions she gives herself to begin and end Act I, "Begin your day, Winnie" (8) and "Pray your old prayer, Winnie" (48) suggest the effort of will that she must exercise to maintain the endless repetition of this circular routine. She calls it doing "all one can." Tersely Winnie also sums up both the problem and the effort required: "There is so little one can say, one says it all" (51).

Even what seems most spontaneous, Winnie's specious reformulation of the *cogito* (I speak; "ergo" you exist to overhear) is less a rationalization than a verbal equivalent of the comic capers of Vladimir and Estragon, intended mainly to keep up morale while passing the time. Winnie's next statement shows that she well knows Willie's presence is unrelated to the sound of her voice (50). He could leave any time, if he has not already. For, despite all her strenuous efforts to continue singing "Happy days are here again" (the song from which the play's title derives), the audience's overall assessment must be that Winnie is singing in the dark. Even Winnie herself concludes that there is "no truth in it anywhere" (51).

Bleak as it first sounds, however, even this statement harbors a saving contradiction. In itself it sounds like a truth, belying its own meaning. Thus, even after saying it, Winnie can continue to be thankful, this time for the "great mercy, all I ask" of incertitude: "not to know, not to know for sure" (51). Winnie's relentless determination to be cheerful, no matter what the circumstances, is her equivalent of Vladimir's determination, against all the evidence, to wait for Godot.

In their different ways both Joyce and Beckett offer us philosophical comedy that challenges our traditional assumptions about the nature of external reality. Joyce's Stephen is ambivalent about rejecting the God of Descartes; the price he pays for such uncertainty about his unbelief is being haunted by his mother's ghost. Beckett's narrators, on the other hand, are haunted by the provisional nature of their own existence. His philosophical comedies demonstrate our desperate attempts to clothe the nudity of nothingness with the illusion of everyday reality, from the tramps waiting for Godot to Winnie's "another happy day" (*HD* 64). Joyce moves in the opposite direction, celebrating his own ability as an artist to exceed reality. Rather than wryly reminding his audience how much his characters lack, as Beckett does, Joyce achieves his own comic effects by encouraging readers to see his narrator trying to make both his characters and what happens to them mean more than they inherently deserve.

Even though they approach the problem differently, both Joyce and Beckett have accepted Descartes' challenge: to explore the paradox of a consciousness having as its object an external world that, experience proves, is both independent of and resistant to such exploration. Critics have often pointed out that Beckett's approach to Descartes (thinking must be prior to being) also makes Beckett a literary exponent of existentialism and of phenomenology.[8] But there is evidence to the contrary: "Once Beckett was asked if his system was the absence of system. He replied, 'I'm not interested in any system. I can't see any trace of any system anywhere'" (Shenker 3).

Here I have placed less emphasis on formal philosophy and more on Beckett's intuitive response to the theological implications of Joyce's fictional technique, elaborating on a contrast suggested in what Shenker has represented as an interview with Beckett (Bair 651 n. 22).

> "In the last book [before this interview]—'L'Innommable'—there's complete disintegration. No 'I,' no 'have,' no 'being,' no nominative, no accusative, no verb. There's no way to go on. . . .
>
> "With Joyce the difference is that Joyce was a superb manipulator of material—perhaps the greatest. He was making words do the absolute maximum of work. There isn't a syllable that's superfluous. The kind of work I do is one in which I'm not master of my material. The more Joyce knew the more he could. He's tending toward omniscience and omnipotence as an artist" [Shenker 1, 3].[9]

Beckett's *The Unnamable* must remain unnamable because it "is that impersonal consciousness which simply 'goes on' thinking and speaking, and which, as such, is always an instant ahead of the namable self which is constituted by its being conscious" (Hesla in Morot-Sir 19). Perhaps this is why, despite the comedy, Beckett's explorations of his characters seem so tortuous. They turn out to be infinite spirals around a self whose existence cannot be adequately explained because it can never be prior to the thought being expressed in the language that articulates it. So Beckett views Joyce's technique as being radically opposed to his own. He excludes and Joyce includes; he underexpresses and Joyce overexpresses. As Beckett moves from creation toward destruction, the artist's failure of silence, Joyce moves "toward omniscience and omnipotence," a return, through narrative "manipulation," to the artist as godlike creator. In contrast, Beckett sums up his own composition of *Endgame* as "'all I can manage, more than I could'" (letter to Alan Schneider, quoted in Bair 470). Yet Beckett's self-proclaimed failure succeeds in affording us critical insight into the nature of Joyce's success. Compared to Beckett, groveling in the muck, Joyce has scaled the Tower of Babel, taking us from the babble at the opening of *Portrait* through the embryonic development of the English language in "Oxen of the Sun," beyond Berlitz to a multinational language suitable for proclaiming his own cosmic myth in *Finnegans Wake.* The Joycean narrator has become a god for whom Christianity is but sacred metaphors, a series of epiphanies suitable for the revelation of his own artistic development.

In his first published story Beckett proposes an artist-hero who comes close to achieving Stephen's dream of being "made not begotten" (*U* 3.45), yet without attaining Stephen's concomitant goal of escaping from history (*U* 2.377). So instead of seeming like an apotheosis, the deification of Beckett's first artist remains static and timebound in its infinite circularity: "'Thus each night he died and was God, each night he revived and was torn, torn and battered with increasing grievousness, so that he hungered to be irretrievably engulfed in the light of eternity'" (quoted in Bair 271). The Joycean analogy between man as artist and God as creator breaks down in Beckett. His fictional narrators (often writers themselves) inevitably fail because their aims are contradictory. The I/eye of their art is fixed and finite in its narrative perspective, whereas their art's object, life itself, is that dynamic process of becoming which remains so unattainable that we have ascribed it to deity. As finite beings we can never capture conceptually (much less in language) the fluidity, dynamism, and comprehensiveness of infinite Being. Joyce's narratives strive to bridge the gap between infinite aspiration and finite performance with a series of rhetorical strategies that become increasingly extroverted, from absence in *Dubliners* to overwhelming presence in *Finnegans Wake*, where the comic texture of the language controls the narrative by calling attention to its own supremacy at every moment. But Beckett's narrative remains introverted, as he makes more out of less through negation. His later short fiction surpasses his former subversion of narrative perspective by undermining language's very location of concepts in time and space. In works like *Imagination Dead Imagine*, *Ping*, *Lessness*, *The Lost Ones*, and *Not I*, "the two-dimensional structure of language itself is all but obliterated in a kaleidoscope of word-fragments endlessly juggled together. There can be . . . no progress of meaning from one statement to the next, no story, no narrator, no fictional world" (Wicker 180). Beckett's increasing cosmological asperity seems an inversion of Joyce's final gesture of plenitude, an unprecedented constriction of meaning in response to the expanding ambiguity of word and world in *Finnegans Wake*.

Yet, for all their different aims and techniques, Joyce and Beckett share a hopefully negative theology. As philosophical tragic-comedians haunted by the loss of ultimacy, they both, like Stephen in "Proteus," turn around to look behind every thing. Yet, even as they turn, the very movement reveals another of Joyce's manipulative narrative strategies, another of Beckett's futile comic "turns." Stephen's parody of Tennyson, the tramps' composite image from popular culture of God as a prudent businessman, and Winnie's dimly recollected snatches of her classics foreshadow no metaphysical future. They remain vacant gestures measuring only the loss of our corporate past. Joyce's and Beckett's profound absurdities seem poignantly appropriate for an age intermittently aware that traditional philosophy has reached its end. Their wit simultaneously diverts us from, and reminds us of, the fact that we can no longer, like Descartes, rely on metaphysics to resolve our ontological dilemmas. The Teller of all Tales has become a fiction. We ought to be forewarned by the excesses of both rhetorical stances, both Joyce's strenuous affirmation of narrative omnipotence and Beckett's desperate denial of it. Even before we turn around, we should suspect what we will find: nothing behind these fictions but ourselves, the readers of our own tale.

Notes

1. Some would deny this account by concentrating on the organization of *Finnegans Wake* rather than on the chaos that is being organized. But the reader's concrete experience of interpreting the language itself, word by word, is far removed from the critic's delineation of whatever overall abstract schemes the symbolic plot comprises. In *Finnegans Wake* the totality of the reading experience is that there can be no totality, only a multiplicity of proliferating alternatives.

2. For example, one critic characterizes *Murphy* as a transitional work which belies its own apparent "assumptions . . . that viable relationships exist among the artist, his art, and the surrounding world, and that complete and absolute structures can be fashioned and communicated." "As traditional as *Murphy*'s form might appear initially, its language, characters, settings, and viewpoints are in fact products of

and consistent with the Beckettian themes presented [of fluidity, uncertainty, and intentional ambiguity]" (Dearlove 15, 26).

3. Perhaps Bloom has sensed Stephen's inner need to communicate and be understood, though, for Bloom next attempts a composition of his own, scratching on the sand a message intended for Gerty MacDowen to find later. Yet he too gets no further than "I. AM. A.," with the curious excuse (considering that he is writing on a vast expanse of beach) that he has "no room" left to continue (*U* 13.1246–65).

4. Before he sees the ship Stephen has already sneered at the Victorian respectability of "Lawn Tennyson" (i.e., a pun on "son of lawn tennis") (*U* 3.490–92; Gifford 47). Since "mother" appears together with "new year" when Stephen thinks about Tennyson, the text he is recollecting must be the opening of "The May Queen": "call me early mother dear; / Tomorrow'll be the happiest time of the glad New-year" (lines 1–2), probably in its setting as a popular song (Gifford 47).

So, with Tennyson recently on his mind, when Stephen sees the ship after having been thinking about a drowned man, he is prepared to recall Tennyson's better-known reference to the new year as the hopeful turning point in *In Memoriam* (stanza 106). Early in that poem Tennyson expressed his grief in an image that merged the movement of the ship with Hallam's body, as if the sea were now doing the breathing for the corpse it contained: "dead calm in that noble breast / Which heaves but with the heaving deep" (stanza 11, lines 19–20). The metaphorical implication that Hallam's mortal energy has been absorbed into the endless rhythms of nature foreshadows the source of consolation announced in terms of the new year. Tennyson is able to reconcile himself to Hallam's death by the end of the poem, seeing it as part of an ultimate convergence between nature's evolutionary process and God's plan, "one far-off divine event, / To which the whole creation moves" (Epilogue, lines 143–44). As poet laureate, this "gentleman poet" has supplied a transcendental view of history which, in the popular mind, can be used to justify British imperialism. As Mr. Deasy had observed to Stephen in the previous chapter, "All human history moves towards one great goal, the manifestation of God" (*U* 2.380–81): and this is the Tennysonian "nightmare from which [Stephen is] trying to awake" (*U* 2.377).

Considering such a subconscious network of religious and political associations, Stephen could be describing the ship in his own mind as Tennyson might, ridiculing his own former credulity with this parody of Tennyson's complacent assurance ("homing, upstream, silently moving" also evokes the mood and imagery of "Crossing the Bar").

5. Earlier in "Proteus" we see an older Stephen mocking the religious aesthetic that he once took so seriously in *Portrait*: "Remember your epiphanies written on green oval leaves, deeply deep, copies to be sent if you died to all the great libraries of the world, including Alexandria?" (*U* 3.141–43). Whether we regard the description of the ship which concludes "Proteus" to come from Stephen himself or from the narrator, it is too unlike both of them in the rest of *Ulysses* to be anything but ironic. The description of the ship must therefore be a satire of Stephen's and Joyce's own former emphasis on *quidditas* as leading to epiphany, Stephen's former belief that the artist can express what is already inherent in the object, its soul or essential reality (*Hendry* 451–52). For it is the very idea of essence residing in being that Stephen questions in this chapter through his inconclusive Cartesian experiment on the beach. Alternatively, we would be agreeing with Marilyn French how remarkable it is that "Stephen, who responds to everything else, makes nothing of [the sailing ship]: he simply sees it" (55).

6. Marilyn French observes that such pure inner monologue causes so much difficulty for the reader because of the removal of "the summarizing phrase, such as 'she thought,'" the removal of the omniscient narrator as a source of truth and value, "the removal of censorship" in terms of subject matter, and "the relaxation of grammatical form" (58–64). But the last page of "Proteus" is replete with phrases like "he said," and I do not believe that the other criteria adequately account for the difficulty here. For "Proteus" I find it more helpful to draw an analogy with reading *The Waste Land*. In both, the consciousness belongs to someone adept at introspection on abstruse subjects and abstract concepts, someone so widely read that he habitually thinks in terms of fragmentary allusions and subtle associations of other thinkers in many disciplines with personal experience. So with both narrators we are being required to decode the shorthand musings of an intellectual who would test our mental agility even in actual conversation when he would be conscious of adapting his interior discourse to the needs of communicating with an audience. The narrators of Beckett's fiction present many of the same difficulties because they tend to be as intellectually allusive as Stephen. In this respect they differ even from Beckett's own central characters in his plays who, while somewhat philosophical, nevertheless draw on a more commonplace frame of reference (Webb 131–32).

7. Stuart Gilbert argues against Professor Curtius' contention that Joyce's analogy breaks down in the relationships between the *leitmotifs* in Joyce's verbal overture and the narrative itself (225–26). But debate over theory does not alter the fact that all Joyce's technical devices reinforcing the analogy between words and music deflect even the most experienced readers' attention from characters and plot toward the narrator's organizational ingenuity.

8. Existential parallels between Beckett and Heidegger and Beckett and Sartre are explored in length in Butler. They are also mentioned more briefly in Hesla, *Shape of Chaos*, which provides the fullest discussion of Beckett and phenomenology, particularly in terms of Husserl and Hegel.

9. Actually the words quoted here are not precisely Beckett's. Shenker both gives and takes away authority in his article: "if [Beckett] would relax his rule on [not granting] interviews, this is what he would say (he has said it all, in precisely this phrasing)." What can "precisely" mean here? When did Beckett "[say] it all"? In a letter to Deirdre Bair (which is not directly quoted either), Bair states, "Shenker said that he had been careful not to say anywhere in the article that he had actually interviewed Beckett, but had used an obvious literary device in order to write it as one long quotation" (Bair 651 n. 22). So did Beckett grant Shenker an interview, then allow him permission to print it on the condition that Shenker not admit it was an interview? Whatever Beckett did or did not do, this is a narrative tangle that might have pleased him—if he had read footnotes.

Works Cited

Bair, Deirdre. *Samuel Beckett, A Biography*. New York: Harcourt Brace Jovanovich, 1978.

Blamires, Harry. *The Bloomsday Book*. London: Methuen, 1966.

Butler, Lance St. John. *Samuel Beckett and the Meaning of Being: A Study in Ontological Parable*. New York: St. Martin's, 1984.

Dearlove, J. E. *Accommodating the Chaos: Samuel Beckett's Nonrelational Art*. Durham: Duke University Press, 1982.

French, Marilyn. *The Book as World: James Joyce's 'Ulysses.'* Cambridge: Harvard University Press, 1976.

Gifford, Don, and Robert J. Seidman. *Notes for Joyce: An Annotation of James Joyce's 'Ulysses.'* New York: Dutton, 1974.

Gilbert, Stuart. *James Joyce's 'Ulysses.'* New York: Knopf, 1930.

Gluck, Barbara Reich. *Beckett and Joyce: Friendship and Fiction.* Lewisburg, Pa.: Bucknell University Press, 1979.

Hendry, Irene. "Joyce's Epiphanies." *The Sewanee Review* 54 (Summer 1946): 449–67.

Herbert, George. *Works.* Rev. ed. F. E. Hutchinson. London: Oxford University Press, 1945.

Hesla, David H. *The Shape of Chaos: An Interpretation of the Art of Samuel Beckett.* Minneapolis: University of Minnesota Press, 1971.

———. "Being, Thinking, Telling, and Loving: The Couple in Beckett's Fiction," *Samuel Beckett: The Art of Rhetoric.* Ed. Edouard Morot-Sir, et al. Chapel Hill: University of North Carolina Press, 1974.

Shenker, Israel. "Moody Man of Letters." *The New York Times* 6 May 1956: sec. 2; 1, 3.

Tennyson, Alfred. *Poems and Plays.* London: Oxford University Press, 1965.

Webb, Eugene. *The Plays of Samuel Beckett.* Seattle: University of Washington Press, 1974.

Wicker, Brian. "Beckett and the Death of the God-Narrator," *The Story-Shaped World: Fiction and Metaphysics, Some Variations on a Theme.* Notre Dame: University of Notre Dame Press, 1975. 169–83.

HERSH ZEIFMAN

The Syntax of Closure: Beckett's Late Drama

In early April of 1981—the exact date was 8 April, coincidentally the same date as the opening of the Beckett conference—I shuffled off to Buffalo to attend the world premiere of Samuel Beckett's latest play, *Rockaby*. I had certainly traveled greater distances in my life to see Beckett on stage (Buffalo is less than a two-hour drive from my home in Toronto), though seldom with greater anticipation. For not only was this a new Beckett work, but it was to be performed by Billie Whitelaw, an actor I deeply admire. My expectations that evening were brilliantly fulfilled; despite its brevity (the play's running time is only about fifteen minutes), I found *Rockaby* to be an extraordinarily moving experience. On one level, my response was purely aesthetic: I'm invariably moved by great acting in the theater, and Whitelaw's performance that night was truly sublime. (As one reviewer rhapsodized: "It's possible that you haven't really lived until you've watched Billie Whitelaw die.")[1] The haunting melodic line of her voice—the heartbreaking intonation, for example, she gave to the repeated refrain "another like herself / a little like"—will live with me forever.[2]

I was also moved, however, on a more personal level: the riveting image of a gray-haired woman rocking away what's left of her life strongly evoked in me the memory of my grandmother ravaged by Alzheimer's, a similarly near-mute figure methodically rocking herself to death. "What is she thinking?" I

From *Beckett On and On . . .* , edited by Lois Oppenheim and Marius Buning, pp. 240–54. Published by Fairleigh Dickinson University Press.

used to wonder as I visited her, hypnotized by that rhythmic rocking to melodies that remained, for me, unheard. Billie Whitelaw, I later discovered, likewise related personally to the character, as she has to all the Beckett women she has portrayed. "Everything [Beckett] writes," she confessed in an interview, "seems to me to be about my life."[3] In the case of *Rockaby*, Whitelaw was reminded specifically of her mother, who in her last five years suffered from Parkinson's: "My mother used to sit in her chair like that, just rocking . . . I used to sit and watch her. I would think, 'Oh, God in heaven, what's going on inside your mind?' . . . How awful it must be to sit there waiting for death."[4]

As I drove back to Toronto after the performance, simultaneously shattered and elated—my usual paradoxical response to a Beckett play—I gradually began to realize that I had been moved by the play on still a third level, and this one perhaps the most profound. "April is the cruellest month," T. S. Eliot begins the first section of *The Waste Land*, "The Burial of the Dead."[5] But though the ending of *Rockaby* seems to me to be about precisely "the burial of the dead," it by no means struck me, that early April evening, as cruel. For the very fact that there is an ending to the play, a resolution—even if that resolution signifies death—is in itself a kind of consolation rarely encountered in Beckett's theater. And it is this act of closure that may be, finally, the most moving element of all in Beckett's late drama.

If we consider briefly the history of drama, it is immediately apparent that the vast majority of plays do come to a definite end; though the exact nature of the resolution may be uncertain and open to debate, a strong sense of closure is nevertheless present. Syntactically, these plays are the equivalent of a periodic sentence. When, for instance, Nora slams the door on her charade of a marriage at the end of *A Doll's House*, we may not be able to foresee the precise reverberations of that slam, but the play still comes to a shuddering stop: the slamming of the door is the "period" that completes the "sentence" of Ibsen's play. While such "periodic" plays are by far the norm, however, the syntax of drama occasionally offers up other constructions. Thus a small group of plays—particularly in the modern theater—ends not on a period but on a question mark: the openness of the ending is built into the play's very structure. The play obviously comes to some kind of close, but genuine closure is denied. Probably the most famous modern play with a "question mark" nonending is Ibsen's *Ghosts*. The hopelessly ill Oswald extracts a promise from his mother that, when the time comes, she will save him from the "living death"[6] of a vegetative existence by giving him an overdose of morphine. In the play's final moments the time has spectacularly come, and yet Mrs. Alving is paralyzed by indecision: can she in effect kill her beloved son? The last words we hear her speak in the play are her attempt to answer that question: "No, no, no!—Yes!—no, no!" The interrogative conclusion of *Ghosts* never resolves that "yes/no": the curtain falls on Mrs. Alving frozen in space, staring at her son "with speechless terror" (p. 128).

An equally small group of plays manages to defy closure through a different syntactical strategy, by "ending" on the equivalent of a colon: a brief pause before the action circles back on itself. What follows the colon is in effect a restatement of the original subject: syntactically, the play's "sentence" never actually ends. The most audacious use in modern drama of this type of nonending is the act 1 close of David Mamet's *Glengarry Glen Ross*, which ends *literally* on a colon: having cornered his hapless prey in the Chinese restaurant that provides the setting of the entire first act, real-estate salesman Ricky Roma moves in for the kill. "Listen to what I'm going to tell you now:" Roma says, the "now" followed on the page by a colon and on the stage by the curtain.[7] Although on the surface the colon functions simply as a signifier of the particular (undramatized) sales pitch Roma uses to hook his victim, it also points to the circularity of the play's overall structure. For while what follows the colon in act 2 seems to provide closure—the criminals who have broken into the real-estate office and stolen valuable information are duly identified and apprehended—that criminal act is ultimately not the play's primary concern. The police investigation of the break-in occurs significantly offstage, in an inner office we never see; what happens meanwhile *onstage*, front and center, is a different sort of "crime" totally ignored by the police: the oxymoronic crime of American business ethics. The last line of the play, Roma's "I'll be at the restaurant" (p. 108), thus returns us appropriately to the scene of the play's beginning. For the structure of *Glengarry Glen Ross* is circular: the apparently climactic discovery of the crooks in fact resolves nothing, because a gang of far more insidious crooks—the corrupt salesmen—is still at large. That the play circles back specifically to a restaurant is symbolically apt, for *Glengarry* is finally a play about consumption—not of food (we never see the salesmen eating) but of people. The "*Practical Sales Maxim*" chosen by Mamet as the play's epigraph, "ALWAYS BE CLOSING" (p. 13), is therefore highly ironic: in this circular play, closure is never attained.

Perhaps the most subtle examples in modern drama of plays that end figuratively on a colon are those of Chekhov. Things certainly happen in a Chekhov play—decisive things, heartbreaking things, things that alter the course of entire lives—and yet, on some important level, nothing important really changes. Such seemingly earth-shattering events as Treplev's suicide in *The Seagull*, or the attempted murder of Serebryakov in *Uncle Vanya*, or the killing of Tuzenbach in *Three Sisters*, or the selling of the estate in *The Cherry Orchard* always occur offstage, anticlimactically—their potential melodrama often deflected into farce, their significance subsumed within the larger, infinitely more mundane tapestry of daily life. There is, then, no genuine resolution at the end of a Chekhov play. His dramas are thus *emotionally*, if not literally, circular: life simply goes on. Consider the close of *Three Sisters*, for instance, which recapitulates the emotional stasis of the opening: the sisters will continue dreaming of a Moscow that will always remain a dream. Most productions of the play stage the sisters' despair at the end as a kind of still-life triptych, the trio frozen in grief and mourning their fate—a decision in accord with Chekhov's stage direction: "*The three sisters stand close to one another.*"[8] When the Czech company Theatre Behind the Gate, however, performed the play in London as part of the 1969 World Theatre Season, director Otomar Krejca made a very different choice: his three sisters expressed their anguish at the end by racing wildly around the stage in what appeared to be a demented frenzy. Almost a quarter of a century later I can still vividly recall those huge circular arcs of despair, those great loops of movement paradoxically going nowhere—an apt description of the structure of the entire play.

It is likewise an apt description, I suggest, of almost all of Beckett's early plays for the theater. The one major exception is *Happy Days*, which subverts closure by means of the alternative syntax: structurally, *Happy Days* has, unusually for Beckett, a "question mark" ending. As Willie attempts to struggle up the mound at the play's close, Winnie is "*Gleeful*"[9]—but "Willie" or won't he ever reach her? In any case, is it indeed Winnie that he wants, or is it rather the revolver "*conspicuous*" by her side (p. 37)? Winnie herself is uncertain:

> Is it me you're after, Willie . . . or is it something else? (Pause.) Do you want to touch my face . . . again? (Pause.) Is it a kiss you're after, Willie . . . or is it something else? (p. 46–47)

Willie's climactic appearance is rendered deliberately ambiguous by Beckett. Attired in "*top hat, morning coat, striped trousers, etc.*," he could be on his way equally to a wedding or to a funeral—an ambiguity further sustained in Beckett's description of him as "*dressed to kill*" (p. 45). Is it the carnal he seeks, then, or the charnel? Winnie has previously informed us of Willie's intense interest in the gun, of how he had begged her to take it away "before I put myself out of my misery" (p. 26). Willie's final word in the play, "Win" (p. 47), is similarly ambiguous. Is he calling out to his wife by name, or is he instead making a horrific pun, implying that death is the only way to "win" at life? The play refuses to answer: *Happy Days* "ends" with the tableau of husband and wife gazing into each other's eyes, but precisely what they see remains in question.

Happy Days aside, the more typical structure of Beckett's early drama is one of circularity.[10] In the fading moments of *Endgame*, Hamm, that ham actor extraordinaire, sensing that the end is near ("It's the end, Clov, we've come to the end" [p. 79]), decides to recite a little poetry: "You prayed—... You CRIED for night; it comes—... It FALLS: now cry in darkness" (p. 83). Despite Hamm's air of spontaneity, the lines, like most of his more lyrical utterances, are not original, though he manages to give them a distinctive twist. The borrowed verse in this instance plucks one of Baudelaire's "fleurs du mal": "Tu réclamais le Soir; il descend; le voici."[11] In Baudelaire the poem is linear, sequential, an answered prayer measured out in semicolons; Hamm's version, significantly, transforms linearity into circularity, the final semicolon now crucially a colon: the lines slither into a tautology, a serpent eating its own tail. "The end is in the beginning," Hamm intuits sorrowfully, "and yet you go on" (p. 69). Like all of Beckett's dramatic characters, the four "pawns" of *Endgame* have indeed cried for "night," for an end to the suffering and wretchedness of their existence. When night finally falls, however, the bitter irony is that nothing has really changed: the longed-for arrival of the end signifies only that there is no "end."

Hamm's rewriting of Baudelaire could stand as an epigraph for the structure of almost all of Beckett's early drama, up to and including *Not I* (1972): to alter slightly the title of Beckett's two mime plays, each of his early plays could have been called "Act Without End." On one level, then, Estragon's summation of the "action" of *Waiting for Godot* is all too cruelly accurate, and not just of that play: "Nothing happens, nobody comes, nobody goes, it's awful"[12]—a cruelty doubled in Vivian Mercier's wicked description of *Godot* as "a play in which nothing happens, *twice*."[13] Beckett's characters wait endlessly, repetitively, for an end that never definitively ends. "Silence and darkness were all I craved," W1 confesses in *Play*;[14] what she craves is in fact what every Beckett character craves: the cessation of words, the cessation of light, the cessation ultimately of play. It is also, paradoxically, what they most fear. "[I]t's time it ended," Hamm states near the beginning of *Endgame*. "And yet I hesitate, I hesitate to ... to end" (p. 3). And when Clov later implores, "Let's stop playing!" Hamm replies, "Never!" (p. 77). It is the same ambivalence experienced by the central figure in Beckett's late prose piece *Stirrings Still*: "Head on hands half hoping when he disappeared again that he would not reappear again and half fearing that he would not."[15]

In Woody Allen's *Annie Hall*, the stand-up comedian played by Allen opens the film by telling a joke that, stripped of its Jewish trappings, is quintessentially Beckettian:

> There's an old joke. Uh, two elderly women are at a Catskills mountain resort, and one of them says: "Boy, the food at this place is really terrible." The other one says: "Yeah, I know, and such ... small portions." Well, that's essentially how I feel about life.[16]

That's essentially how Beckett's characters feel about life, too; strange as it may at first sound, Allen and Beckett share—up to a point—a similar comic sensibility. "Nothing is funnier than unhappiness" (p. 18), Nell reminds us in *Endgame* in what is, for Beckett, the most important line in the play.[17] But Allen's black humor becomes infinitely blacker in Beckett, the pain far more deeply felt. For Beckett's characters, life is simultaneously utterly wretched and wretchedly brief; yearning for an end, they nevertheless resent the inevitable end of yearning. As Beckett remarked in *Proust*: "The mortal microcosm cannot forgive the relative immortality of the macrocosm. The whisky bears a grudge against the decanter."[18]

Whether desired or feared, however—or, rather, *both* desired *and* feared—the end, when it finally arrives in Beckett's plays, is never-ending, never final. "I don't seem to be able . . . to depart," Pozzo concludes in the first act of *Godot*; "Such is life," responds Estragon (p. 47). Similarly, while *Endgame* closes with Clov "*dressed for the road*," in the final tableau he remains trapped on the stage, "*impassive and motionless*" (p. 82). "This is what we call making an exit" (p. 81), Clov stated previously as he attempted to depart; in actuality, though, nobody in Beckett's early drama is ever permitted to make a genuine exit. For where is there to go, except back to the very beginning? The circle, by definition, denies closure. In this, as in many other ways (their extensive use of subtext, for example), Beckett's early plays recall Chekhov's: they too "end" on a figurative colon, a pause before the same action—literally or metaphorically—resumes yet again. Structurally, they are the dramatic equivalent of the illuminated Bovril sign described so outrageously in Beckett's short story "A Wet Night": when the seven gaudy phases of the sign's cycle come to an end, the cycle automatically begins once more—"*Da capo*."[19] Beckett's early drama might thus be termed—to coin a suitably Joycean bilingual pun—*palindrames*: plays that "read" the same backwards as forwards. Except, of course, it's never quite the same: the "backwards" reading of a Beckett text is always slightly yet significantly different from the "forwards" reading, precisely because we have previously read it. The fact that nothing happens twice in Beckett's early drama, then, is on one level the something that happens.

The circularity of Beckett's theater, the repeated denial of closure, creates in effect a trap from which there is no escape: as there is no end to the play, so there is no end to the play of human suffering. The show, in a horrifyingly literal sense, must go on. The most relentless example of this circularity in Beckett is his 1963 drama, *Play*. On the surface, the three characters buried in urns appear to be in the same position as Dante's Belacqua, the Antepurgatory figure described by Beckett in *Murphy* as "immune from expiation until he should have dreamed [his life] all through again, . . . from the spermarium to the crematorium, . . . before the toil uphill to Paradise."[20] The significant difference is that Beckett's cosmography lacks a Paradise. The characters of *Play* relive the details of their earthly lives *endlessly*; for them, there is no possibility of "expiation," no possibility of closure. Thus, at the "end" of *Play*, Beckett directs that the entire play should be repeated, and the curtain finally falls on the beginning of yet another repetition: specifically, on M's line: "We were not long together" (p. 61).[21] The irony here is doubly exquisite: this eternal triangle is in fact doomed to be together *eternally*, and at the same time doomed never to be *together*—the incorporeal "lines" of their triangle never intersect. The impossibility of a climax in Beckett's drama, in any sense of the word, ultimately becomes as frustrating *theatrically* as it would be sexually. The circular structure of Beckett's early theater is therefore profoundly anti-erotic, regardless of its particular subject matter. For endless repetition invariably creates an unbearable tension in the audience—a tension that, lacking closure, can never find release.

Release is similarly denied in Beckett's *Not I*: trapped in the unyielding glare of a circular spotlight, Mouth ends the play still desperately seeking the "right" words to say, words that will "free" her and bring her torment to a close. No such closure is possible, however, because no such words exist: like Lucky's "think," Mouth's monologue is a round dance of futility that could go on indefinitely. Lucky's unpunctuated monologue "ends" solely because he is attacked and physically forced to keep silent (significantly "finishing" on the word "unfinished" [p. 45]); Mouth's logorrhea, also unpunctuated, likewise "ends" solely because the curtain falls and cuts her off (though she continues to speak, unintelligibly, for a further ten seconds, ceasing only when the house lights come up).[22] The circularity of *Not I*, then, once more resists closure. The actor portraying Mouth never actually leaves the stage, but rather the reverse: the stage leaves the actor.

In the quartet of theater plays that immediately follow *Not I*, however, we note a startling stylistic shift: gradually, almost imperceptibly, Beckett's late minimalist drama inches its way towards a kind of closure. All four plays feature a single onstage character (though only one is truly a monologue); all four characters are literally eccentric, placed deliberately "*off centre.*" In *That Time* (1976), the character is Listener, a disembodied face floating ten feet above stage level, listening to a trinity of voices (his own voice split into three) replaying memories of three different stages of his life. The surface similarity to *Not I* is obvious; indeed, Beckett told Patrick Magee, who originated the role of Listener, that he would never allow the two plays to be performed on the same bill: *That Time*, according to Beckett, was too clearly "cut out of the same texture as *Not I*."[23] And yet, despite their similarity, *That Time* provides a brief flicker of hope, a subtle hint of closure, absent from *Not I*. Like all of Beckett's drama, the play attempts to move from "that time" (its opening words) to "no time" (its closing words)—attempts, that is, to attain closure by bridging the gap between them, in effect obliterating time. And like many of Beckett's protagonists, Listener both yearns for this closure and simultaneously fears it: as [Voice] B notes, Listener's "stories" are designed "to keep the void out just another of those old tales to keep the void from pouring in on top of you the shroud." In *That Time*, however—for the first time in Beckett's theater—the "shroud" may actually be allowed to blanket the play's ending; the possibility of dramatic closure seems, this time, finally within reach.

That Time is divided into three brief "acts," each act followed by a ten-second silence in which the voices are momentarily stilled. As the play progresses, the movement towards closure, towards "no time," becomes more and more urgent, culminating in its last speech, a dirge in which [Voice] C mourns the transience of human existence and his own mortality by evoking the words of "the dust":

> what was it it said come and gone was that it something like that come and gone come and gone no one come and gone in no time gone in no time

In the ritualistic silence that ensues, the play's seemingly infinite pattern is suddenly shattered: after three seconds, Listener's eyes open, as usual, but this is followed two seconds later by an inscrutable "*smile*," held for five seconds until the final fade-out and curtain. That smile, though ambiguous—perhaps scornful, perhaps suffused with happiness, perhaps both—brings the play to a dramatic halt, presumably stilling the voices once and for all: the rest is silence. When Beckett directed *That Time* in Berlin, he deliberately slowed down the last speech in each "act," the play's final speech being the slowest of all. "[R]emember the ritardando at the end of Parts I, II and III," he instructed Klaus Herm, who was playing Listener. "Above all," he continued, "at the very end a dramatic effect should be achieved: 'will it go on again.'"[24] In *That Time*, the tension surrounding closure appears to be resolved: mercifully, the play does not go on again. *That Time* finally seems to have embraced "no time": no more words; no more light; no more "play."

In *Footfalls* (1976), the onstage character is May—a character who has not quite been born, who only *may* exist, who wears, according to Beckett, "the costume of a ghost."[25] As the play opens, we see her dimly lit figure obsessively pacing back and forth along a narrow strip at the front of the stage, listening to the sounds of her footfalls, "revolving it all" in her mind. The strip is about the size of a cemetery plot; May is thus, in a sense, pacing her own grave. Significantly, May begins her "revolution" by walking from right to left; as the protagonist of *How It Is* comments, "and death in the west as a rule."[26] Like so many of Beckett's characters, May is embarked on a long day's journey into night: westward, though not necessarily worstward, ho. Is such closure, however, capable of being attained? "Will you never have done . . . revolving it all?" the voice of May's offstage mother muses aloud—the question implicitly asked of all of Beckett's characters. Like *That Time*, *Footfalls* appears to be divided into three brief "acts," each act a diminution, a *cascando*, of the preceding one: the faint chime that opens the acts becomes progressively fainter, the dim light progressively dimmer, May's slow pacing progressively slower. But *Footfalls*, even more than *That Time*, carries a surprising sting in its tail. For there is a *fourth* "act" to this play—a startling "coda" composed equally of "silence and darkness": as the chime sounds a little fainter, the light, likewise a little dimmer, fades up to reveal "*No trace of MAY.*" May has simply disappeared—in Billie Whitelaw's words, "spiralling inward, inward." "I said to Sam," Whitelaw further remarked, "that as the light goes he should have only a little pile of fuller's earth. There is nothing left."[27] The "imprisoned" Clov, frozen in the tableau of *Endgame*'s cyclical endlessness, could only dream of the liberation granted the finally absent May: *this* is what we call making an exit![28]

The speaker of Beckett's *A Piece of Monologue* (1979)—"*White hair, white nightgown, white socks*"—is on a similar journey, though he never once moves during the course of the play: a journey from "Birth," the first word in the play, to its last word, "gone," a journey towards closure. Journey's end is signaled in its beginning: "Birth was the death of him," the speaker notes. "Birth" is thus the "rip" word that embodies its own demise: r.i.p. (rest in peace); "the word go" inevitably becomes "The word begone." Yet "silence and darkness," while always hovering at the edge of the frame, seem to lie tantalizingly just outside the speaker's grasp. Thus, when he remembers "Faint sounds" and comments "None now," he immediately corrects himself: "No. No such thing as none"; his parallel conclusion about the "Light dying," "Soon none left to die," is likewise instantly emended: "No. No such thing as no light." Paradoxically, this monologist is not alone on stage: "*Two metres to his left, same level, same height,* [*is a*] *standard lamp, skull-sized white globe, faintly lit.*" As Mel Gussow has noted, the lamp becomes the speaker's "silent, totemic double. . . . Any second we expect [it] to speak."[29] Thirty seconds before the speaker reaches his last word, "gone," the lamplight begins to go; at play's end, Beckett's stage directions read: "*Lamp out. Silence.*" The light slowly fading in that "*skull-sized white globe*" is one of the most haunting images of closure in Beckett's late drama. And yet, *A Piece of Monologue* backtracks slightly from the more definitive closure of *Footfalls*. For the dying of the light does not result in total darkness: the speaker and globe, Beckett notes, are still "*barely visible in diffuse light.*" To find the most powerful instance of closure in the Beckett canon, we need instead to turn to Beckett's next stage play, *Rockaby*.

Rockaby (1981) brilliantly encapsulates the central images of the entire quartet of these late Beckett plays: while "*revolving* it all," her chair steadily rocking into and out of the light, W, the play's protagonist, both *listens* to her own recorded voice (V) crooning a lullaby of eternal sleep and occasionally *speaks* two apparently contradictory phrases: "More," repeated four times, and "time she stopped," repeated seven times. The contradiction is only apparent, for W's "More" is in reality "less," a way of propelling herself towards nothingness: we have been on this journey before. The lullaby V croons modulates imperceptibly into a threnody, a rhythmically incantatory verse that begins midsentence without a capital letter and ends, appropriately on the word "off," without a period—"an extended predicate," Jonathan Kalb has noted, "that refuses to resolve."[30] Like most of Beckett's late drama, the play is divided into a number of brief "acts," each preceded by W's imploring "More," each a deeper descent into silence and darkness. Thus the light becomes progressively a little fainter; the voices of both W and V become a little softer; W's eyes gradually begin to close; the rocking chair ultimately comes to a halt.

Defiantly dressed for closure in her "best black"—a lacy, sequined evening gown with "incongruous frivolous headdress"—W sits at play's end blind, mute, completely immobile. Her last words, "rock her off / rock her off," have become both an auditory and visual pun: she is now truly "off her rocker"; the "rocker" is now permanently "off." If "time she stopped" has been the recurrent leitmotif in this lullaby of stopping, we finally comprehend the double meaning of that haunting and ambiguous phrase. For W's decision that it is time to stop is dramatized in the end by her *stopping time*: rock is stilled; voice is silent; there is literally no "More." As the lights fade, we see her head slowly sink and come to rest—the theatrical period noticeably absent from the text as verse narrative. There is no more moving emblem of closure in all of Beckett's late drama.

When I speak of Beckett's late drama ultimately achieving closure, I by no means wish to imply that a Beckett text is thereby somehow "closed," reducible to a single, fixed meaning—the kind of text that Roland Barthes calls "lisible." On the contrary, Beckett's theater is, in Barthes's terminology, remarkably "scriptible": there is always an open play of possibilities in Beckett, a "galaxy of signifiers" that constitutes a genuinely plural significance. Beckett's drama thus embodies what is for Barthes the goal of all literary work: "to make the reader no longer a consumer but a producer of the text."[31] By closure, rather, I mean only this sense of resolution we discover—however we may choose to interpret it—at the end of Beckett's late drama. The *desire* for such closure—"for to end yet again"—is clearly nothing new in Beckett's work: its urgency pulses through his writing from exuberant beginning to weary close. The protagonist of *Stirrings Still*, for example—one of the last pieces Beckett wrote—is engaged in the same age-old quest: "patience till the one true end to time and grief and self and second self his own" (p. 11). The Shakespearean echo in the phrase "second self" clarifies precisely what the protagonist is awaiting: in Sonnet 73, Shakespeare writes of "black night . . . , / Death's second self that seals up all in rest."[32] It is what every Beckett protagonist is awaiting, and simultaneously dreading: the closing of the book.

What is different in Beckett's late drama is thus only a tiny, though momentous, shift of emphasis—the shift from "Little is left to tell," the opening words of *Ohio Impromptu*, to "Nothing is left to tell," the words that bring that play to a close. It is the difference, in short, between "stirrings still"—there is movement yet—and "stirrings still," the cessation of movement; between simple alliteration and profound oxymoron; between the last gasp of life and the first grasp of death. The tenuously precarious balance of a Beckett play has finally tilted, and the tilt is reflected in a change of syntax: abandoning the endless circularity of the colon, Beckett metaphorically puts a period to his writing. All that has really happened is that the shape of a Beckett text has ever so slightly altered—but then, as Beckett reminds us, "It is the shape that matters."[33]

In a much-quoted interview with Tom Driver in 1961, Beckett reportedly remarked:

> If there were only darkness all would be clear. . . . But where we have both dark and light we have also the inexplicable. The key word in my plays is "perhaps."[34]

Perhaps that judgment was valid for Beckett's plays before *Not I*: since then, however, the "yes-no's of yesteryear"—to borrow an outrageous pun from Tom Stoppard's *Travesties*[35]—have long since melted away. In any case, that "perhaps" was always the longest of shots in Beckett's drama, one of its most cruel ironies. Perhaps Godot will eventually come; perhaps the "endgame" will one day progress to "checkmate"; perhaps the spotlight in *Play* will finally go out. As we have seen, the structure of Beckett's early plays consistently denies such closure; if we continued to hope, it was only because to abandon all hope, as Dante reminds us, is to enter hell. And Beckett's drama, like the Joycean universe he described in his essay in *Our Exagmination*, seemed so obviously "purgatorial" in its "absolute absence of the Absolute."[36]

In his final decade of playwriting, however, Beckett's drama gradually moved closer to an acceptance of the Absolute, or at least its "relative presence." In the now almost unbearably poignant documentary film of the making of *Rockaby*, the late Alan Schneider explained his interpretation of the play to Billie Whitelaw: "It's not about dying. It's not about coming to die. It's about accepting—*accepting* death."[37] Beckett spent almost his entire writing career both acknowledging the inevitability of death and railing against its acceptance. So too did the poet Philip Larkin; in "Aubade," for example, one of Larkin's last, uncollected poems, the dread of dying still "Flashes afresh to hold and horrify":

> Being brave
> Lets no one off the grave.
> Death is no different whined at than withstood.
>
> Slowly light strengthens, and the room takes shape.
> It stands plain as a wardrobe, what we know,
> Have always known, know that we can't escape,
> Yet can't accept.[38]

Ironically, "Aubade" turns out to be a threnody: the light of dawn serves only to make clear the final sunset that must inevitably follow—a sunset from which the poet resolutely turns away. Beckett also wrote aubades that were in reality threnodies—like "Alba" and "Da Tagte Es," poems that appeared in his 1935 collection *Echo's Bones*. But whereas Larkin's poem dates from 1977, less than a decade before his death, Beckett's work by then—in its shift to the syntax of closure—had long since unflinchingly refused to turn away.

On one of my last visits before her death, my grandmother, who for the previous year had talked not at all or only gibberish, suddenly uttered a coherent sentence; speaking to me in Yiddish—or to herself, or perhaps, like W in *Rockaby*, simply to the rocking chair—she whispered: "We make peace with fate." It takes courage to make that peace, especially when our fate, as Vladimir reminds us in Godot, is "cruel" (p. 79) and the peace inevitably Pyrrhic. Beckett's writing has always been courageous—the perfect exemplar of Kurt Vonnegut's definition of high art: "Making the most of the raw materials of futility"[39]—but never more so than in his late plays, where futility is at last allowed to triumph. The movement towards closure in Beckett's late drama—even if it denotes a journey into the void, a journey to an "unspeakable home"[40]—thus resolves an enormous tension in both Beckett's characters and his audiences. For if Hamm's repeated summation of human existence is correct—"You're on earth, there's no cure for that!" (pp. 53, 68)—if the light of salvation is indeed "extinguished" (p. 42) or, worse, merely a mocking "trick" of the light—then to achieve total darkness becomes a blessing, a kind of redemption. During rehearsals of *Endgame* in Berlin, Beckett commented to his actors: "Hamm sagt das Nein gegen das Nichts" (Hamm says No to nothingness);[41] courageously, movingly, the woman in *Rockaby* rocks herself to a resounding yes. In Beckett's late plays, the "silence and darkness" his characters so desperately crave, the transition from "that time" to "no time," is finally, mercifully, attained.[42]

Notes

1. Frank Rich, quoted in Barbara Lovenheim, "A Canvas Who Has Lost Her Paintbrush," *New York Times*, 2 September 1990, H5.

2. Because Beckett's late plays tend to be so brief, specific page numbers will not be cited in the text. The late plays from which I quote are all published in *Collected Shorter Plays of Samuel Beckett* (London: Faber & Faber, 1984): *That Time*, pp. 225–35; *Footfalls*, pp. 237–43; *A Piece of Monologue*, pp. 263–69; *Rockaby*, pp. 271–82; and *Ohio Impromptu*, pp. 283–88.

3. Billie Whitelaw interviewed by Linda Ben-Zvi, in Linda Ben-Zvi, ed., *Women in Beckett: Performance and Critical Perspectives* (Urbana: University of Illinois Press, 1990), p. 3.

4. Billie Whitelaw, quoted in David Edelstein, "Rockaby Billie," *Village Voice*, 20 March 1984, 81; and in Mel Gussow, "Billie Whitelaw's Guide to Performing Beckett," *New York Times*, 14 February 1984, 21.

5. T. S. Eliot, *The Waste Land*, in *Selected Poems* (London: Faber, 1962), p. 51.

6. Henrik Ibsen, *Ghosts*, trans. R. Farquharson Sharp, in John Gassner, ed., *Four Great Plays by Ibsen* (New York: Bantam, 1971), p. 108.

7. David Mamet, *Glengarry Glen Ross* (New York: Grove, 1984), p. 51.

8. Anton Chekhov, *Three Sisters*, trans. Ann Dunnigan, in Robert Brustein, ed., *Chekhov: The Major Plays* (New York: Signet, 1964), p. 311.

9. Samuel Beckett, *Happy Days* (London: Faber, 1966), p. 46.

10. On another level, however, *Happy Days* is not really atypical, since it can be argued that the overall structure of the play is indeed circular: act 2 essentially repeats, mutatis mutandis, the "action" of act 1. The mound of earth in which Winnie is progressively buried thus evokes the Zenoist "impossible heap" alluded to in *Endgame*, a heap that can never attain completion. See Samuel Beckett, *Endgame* (New York: Grove, 1958), p. 70.

11. Charles Baudelaire, "Recueillement," in *Les fleurs du mal*, ed. J. Crépet and G. Blin (Paris: Corti, 1942), p. 195.

12. Samuel Beckett, *Waiting for Godot* (London: Faber, 1965), p. 41.

13. Vivian Mercier, *Beckett/Beckett* (New York: Oxford University Press, 1977), p. xii.

14. Samuel Beckett, *Play, Cascando and Other Short Dramatic Pieces* (New York: Grove, 1970), p. 59.

15. Samuel Beckett, *Stirrings Still* (New York: Blue Moon; London: Calder, 1988), p. 4.

16. Woody Allen and Marshall Brickman, *Annie Hall*, in *Four Films of Woody Allen* (London: Faber, 1983), p. 4.

17. See Ruby Cohn, *Just Play: Beckett's Theater* (Princeton: Princeton University Press, 1980), p. 243.

18. Samuel Beckett, *Proust* (London: John Calder, 1965), pp. 21–22.

19. Samuel Beckett, "A Wet Night," in *More Pricks Than Kicks* (New York: Grove, 1970), p. 47.

20. Samuel Beckett, *Murphy* (London: John Calder, 1963), p. 56.

21. When Beckett attended rehearsals for the French production of *Play* (*Comédie*) in 1964, directed by Jean-Marie Serreau, he introduced some variation—specifically, "a slight weakening"—to the exact repetition of the text, thus producing a sense of "falling off . . . , with suggestion of conceivable dark and silence in the end, or of an indefinite approximating towards it. . . ." See Beckett's letter to George Devine, dated 9 March 1964, in John Knowlson, ed., *Samuel Beckett: An Exhibition* (London: Turret, 1971), p. 92.

22. Samuel Beckett, *Not I* (London: Faber, 1973), pp. 15–16.

23. Quoted in Enoch Brater, *Beyond Minimalism: Beckett's Late Style in the Theater* (New York: Oxford University Press, 1987), p. 37. See also Cohn, *Just Play*, p. 30.

24. Quoted in Walter D. Asmus, "Practical Aspects of Theatre, Radio and Television: Rehearsal Notes for the German Premiere of Beckett's *That Time* and *Footfalls* at the Schiller-Theater Werkstatt, Berlin (directed by Beckett)," trans. Helen Watanabe, *Journal of Beckett Studies* 2 (1977): 92, 94.

25. Quoted in ibid., p. 85. When Billie Whitelaw asked Beckett if May was dead, Beckett replied, "Let's just say you're not quite there." Quoted in Jonathan Kalb, *Beckett in Performance* (Cambridge: Cambridge University Press, 1989), p. 235. See also Gussow, "Billie Whitelaw's Guide," p. 21.

26. Samuel Beckett, *How It Is* (London: John Calder, 1964), p. 134.

27. Quoted in Ben-Zvi, *Women in Beckett*, p. 9.

28. See Brater, *Beyond Minimalism*, p. 60.

29. Mel Gussow, "Beckett Distills His Vision," *New York Times*, 31 July 1983, H3.

30. Kalb, *Beckett in Performance*, p. 12.

31. Roland Barthes, *S/Z* (Paris: Editions du Seuil, 1970), pp. 9–12 (my translations).

32. William Shakespeare, *The Sonnets*, in *Shakespeare: The Complete Works*, ed. G. B. Harrison (New York: Harcourt, 1968).

33. Quoted in Harold Hobson, "Samuel Beckett, Dramatist of the Year," in *International Theatre Annual No. 1* (London: John Calder, 1956), p. 153.

34. Tom Driver, "Beckett by the Madeleine," *Columbia University Forum* 4, no. 3 (1961): 23.

35. Tom Stoppard, *Travesties* (London: Faber, 1975), p. 25.

36. Samuel Beckett, "Dante . . . Bruno. Vico . . Joyce," in *Our Exagmination Round his Factification for Incamination of Work in Progress*, 1929, rpt. in Samuel Beckett, *Disjecta: Miscellaneous Writings and a Dramatic Fragment*, ed. Ruby Cohn (New York: Grove, 1984), p. 33.

37. *Rockaby*, directed by D. A. Pennebaker and Chris Hegedus, Pennebaker Associates, 1982.

38. Philip Larkin, "Aubade," *Times Literary Supplement* 23 (December 1977): 1491.

39. Kurt Vonnegut, *Hocus Pocus* (New York: Berkeley, 1991), p. 14.
40. See Beckett's poem "neither," *Journal of Beckett Studies* 4 (1979): v.
41. Quoted in Cohn, *Just Play*, p. 241.
42. Some of the issues raised in this paper were first explored (more briefly and tentatively) in a short paper I delivered at the "Beckett and Beyond" conference, Princess Grace Irish Library, Monaco, May 1991. See also my article "'The Core of the Eddy': *Rockaby and Dramatic Genre*," in Friedman, Rossman, and Sherzer, eds., *Beckett Translating/Translating Beckett* (University Park: Pennsylvania State University Press, 1987), pp. 140–48.

GIUSEPPINA RESTIVO

Caliban/Clov and Leopardi's Boy: Beckett and Postmodernism

Beckett and *The Tempest*

The Tempest is recurrently present in Beckett's theatre. In *Waiting for Godot* 'the divine Miranda' is mentioned in Lucky's monologue, while *Endgame* produces the direct quotation of a line from Act IV, Scene 1 of Shakespeare's play, 'our revels now are ended', less evident in the original French *Fin de partie*. But this is not, as one might think, Beckett's only quotation from *The Tempest* in *Endgame*.

The chess game hinted at in the title of the play is indeed a multiple quotation. It leads back to Marcel Duchamp, Beckett's friend and chess expert, author of a treatise on special cases of 'endgame', in which the outcomes of the third and final phase of a game of chess are analysed; but it also echoes the enigmatic chess game in Shakespeare's *Tempest*, evoked in Hamm's words from Prospero's 'our revels' passage, and already 'actualised' in T. S. Eliot's reference to *The Tempest* and his chess game metaphor in *The Waste Land*. Eliot is indeed present in *Endgame*, *The Hollow Men* being echoed in Hamm's last monologue as I have shown elsewhere, in a comparison between Beckett's desert and Eliot's waste.[1] Yet not even the double hint at the masque and the chess game in *The Tempest* exhausts the connection between the two texts, a connection of a larger, deeper, ironical nature.

Repeating Prospero's words 'our revels now are ended', Beckett's Hamm directly opposes his own and Clov's paradoxical 'entertaining unhappiness' to

---

From *Beckett and Beyond,* edited by Bruce Stewart, pp. 217-30. Published by Colin Smythe.

the Utopian masque used by Prospero in *The Tempest*, as a device to complete Ferdinand's ideal education, while celebrating his marriage to Miranda. This is more than cursory memory: it is indeed a confrontation as deeply-rooted as Beckett's text itself, that repeats from Shakespeare's play the educational relationship between a servant and his master, who has raised him since a child. It even repeats the servant's rebellion: like Caliban, Clov wants freedom from his master. The Hamm/Clov relationship actually seems to condense the Prospero/Miranda or father/child relationship as well, and somehow to refer to the Ferdinand/Miranda relation for, as Beckett himself pointed out, it includes any couple's relationship. The interplay of analogies and reversals is complex.

In Prospero's plans the 'revels' exhibited in the masque are a symbolic program and a Utopian representation on which are based the plans for a regenerated history; in Hamm's words the 'revels' are a hint at the narcissistic exchanges between Hamm and Clov, to the point of perverse sado-masochistic drives and 'double bind' constrictions,[2] reflecting Beckett's experience of psychoanalysis at the Tavistock Clinic in London with R. W. Bion, for a year and a half, in 1934/1935. In Beckett, Utopia is substituted with what the author called *dianoia*, a 'knowing through' of the workings of the inner self, that entrap relationships and lead to anguish and self-torture. According to Didier Anzieu, Beckett relevantly influenced Bion in his psychoanalytical theories.[3]

As to the game of chess, it appears as a model for relationships in both plays. In Act V, Scene 1 of *The Tempest*, Ferdinand 'plays false' to Miranda, but she justifies her newly-married husband's ways both out of love and referring to the worldly interests that the future king will have to foster. The implication is that manipulation or fight are acceptable in terms of power and government, not within the couple. Two different lines of behaviour are therefore envisaged. Quoting Montaigne's essay *Les cannibales* and preceding by a century Rousseau's *Emile*, the play shows a new prince, Ferdinand, who has been reeducated by Prospero—on his magic island and on the country-like background emphasised in the fiction of his masque—to a primacy of natural positiveness and love over political interests as regards the couple. But with the chess game the prince is then led to deal properly with a compound of idyllic-Utopian enlightenment and the Renaissance sense of state and history.[4]

The balance between Utopia and history exhibited by Shakespeare through the illusion of what Prospero calls 'my so potent art', magic (or hypnotic) means and 'word representation', is indeed incompatible with Beckett's outlook. In Beckett's eyes the chess game—seen as the structural model of any relationship—has become a relentless interplay of trivial war games, excluding love and producing suffering, on the background of a common wait for the end, already a central theme in *En attendant Godot*. No Utopia is left here, not even as an illusory or heuristic ideal: in this sense *Endgame* is a reversed double of *The Tempest*.

But the relationship between Beckett's and Shakespeare's plays may extend even farther. A third more cryptic 'interference' may be found between the two: Clov's very name might be repeating Caliban's, implying a more pervasive connection.

According to Enoch Brater, Clov's name can be linked to the Hebrew word for dog, *kelev*, and certainly there is large textual evidence for such a meaning in the play, possibly even a link with the dog in Dürer's *Melencolia*.[5] But Caliban's name too may actually derive—as Roger Toumson has pointed out in an essay on *The Tempest*,[6] using Ernest Renan's *Histoire du peuple d'Israël*—from a Hebrew-Arabian source, as meaning 'God's dog' or 'dog's head', the same source providing the names Ariel, Sycorax (the witch from Algiers) and Setebos as well. Probably a mixture of Hebrew Caleb or Calebel and the French 'cannibale', from the title of Montaigne's essay *Les cannibales*, Caliban's name seems to share a derivation common with Clov's. Both dog-servants in role and name, Caliban and Clov actually perform the same *récit* of language-dependence and language-rebellion with regard to their masters, positing the double problem of word and world control. Clov has been taught language by Hamm, and protests for the uselessness of words—contesting for instance the meaning of the word 'yesterday'—just as Caliban denounces his linguistic education by Prospero, that only allows him to curse his master.

Moreover, while analysing the uses of the name Caleb connected with the Hebrew word for dog, Ernest Renan mentions a Caleb who followed Moses into the desert and reached the promised land as indicated in the *Pentateuch*: but the *Pentateuch* is a text that the genesis of *Endgame* shows as one of its main sources. In an early two-act version of *Fin de partie*, Clov reads a long passage from the *Pentateuch*, and the word *Pentateuch* is at the centre of comical transformations in Clov's pronunciation:

> B—*Un peu de* Pentatuque?
> A—*De quoi?*
> B—*Pentatuque.*
> A—*Tatuque! Tateuque.* Pentateuque.
> B—*Comment?*
> A—*Ta*teuque. *Penta*teuque. Pentatuque!
> B—*Teuque ou tuque, tu en veux, oui ou merde?*
> A—*N'importe quoi, je te dis! Le Déluge!*[7]

This passage was later deleted, but a new passage was then added at the end of the play, where the biblical relation Caleb or Clov/Moses is introduced. Clov wants to leave Hamm and abandon his refuge, in front of which a boy seems to have suddenly appeared, and in the French *Fin de partie* the boy is described as having '*les yeux de Moise mourant*'. Like the biblical Caleb mentioned by Renan, Clov aims at Moses and at the myth of salvation from the desert, though with a total ironical reversal. Clov indeed wants to kill the Moses-boy with a gaff, while Hamm halts him, and will reach no promised land: he actually dresses as if he were to leave the refuge, but remains motionless and silent by blind Hamm's chair. This will eventually lead them both to death.

The link between *The Tempest* and *Endgame* appears then as multiple, implying not only the obvious 'revels passage', or the chess game, but a closer link between Clov and Caliban, cutting through the structure of Beckett's play and its central opposition between a master and a servant. If Caliban is finally freed by a departing Prospero, and solves his love–hatred relationship with him by acknowledging his master's qualities, Beckett's apparently departing Clov does not change his repetitive love–hatred attitude towards his master: *Endgame* actually evokes the *récit* of *The Tempest* in order to 'falsify' it, to construe its 'impossibility'.

But the interplay does not end here either: it ranges even beyond the radical criticism of reversal. It in fact produces a *double falsification*: of Shakespeare's *récit* as of its own reversal. It does not imply a Dadaistic or an iconoclastic gesture, but a postmodern 'dianoia'.

Shakespeare's Utopian fable is indeed 'falsified' by Beckett's 'absurd' reversal in *Endgame* at the same time as Beckett's own *récit* is finally falsified by its very author: the end of the play shows that the lifeless condition of the world outside the two protagonists' refuge, on the assumption of which their relationship is based, must be false. In W. Bion's terms the description of the context appears as a *pseudos*, a self-deception enacted on the paradoxical basis of an incapability to dismiss a lie, although aware of it. Beckett's dystopia is so revealed as 'unnecessary' as Prospero's Utopia: if on the one hand Beckett criticises Shakespeare's choice, on the other he criticises his own criticism, apparently defeating one aim with another.

But if seen through Juri Lotman's theory of cultural codes, this strange complex link between the two plays, *The Tempest* and *Endgame*, can better yield the meaning of its profound inner 'necessity'. The negation of both *récits* can in fact be explained not as a sarcastic culture-effacing double destruction, but as today's necessary exploration of the two different possible outcomes of one code our culture is heir to, exposed in the link between the two plays. The code central to both texts—that Lotman defines as both 'synchronic' and historically dominant in the age of enlightenment, and ever since combined or opposed to the code of romanticism[8]—is taken by Beckett to its extremities to the point of self- criticism.[9]

If, through Montaigne's influence, Shakespeare's *récit* anticipates 18th century Utopian planning of a 'new history' and its code, Beckett's *counter-récit* implies a wider range of implications.

On the one hand it evokes Shakespeare, on the other it echoes and radicalises the scepticism of two 18th century authors, Dr Johnson (as pointed out by Ruby Cohn), and Chamfort, a reference still to be explored. One of Chamfort's maxims in particular was by Beckett used twice—in French and in English—as an inscription to a personal copy of *Endgame* donated to a friend, and was then repeatedly quoted by Beckett on different occasions. Compounding reference to Shakespeare as well as to Johnson or Chamfort, Beckett actually appears to be staging what Lotman calls the 'double outcome', the Utopian and the absurd versions of the code of enlightenment, in a thorough exploration of this code, based on 'desemiotisation', as such open to absolute freedom and possible alternatives to history, but also exposed to a sense of deprivation of meaning and the total illusoriness of Utopia as of any representation.

Beckett's full philosophical awareness of the consequences of his dianoia then brings him on the verge of a postmodern 'beyond', on the brink of which Clov halts, as in the final scene of the play.

In this view, Beckett's position appears to restate, for our century and at a further level, the same philosophical problem posed at the close of the age of enlightenment during the first decades of the 19th century by an author he much admired and quoted in his essay on Proust: Giacomo Leopardi, one of the major voices of Italian literature. European in culture and polyglot to the point of a masterful use of Italian and German, not to mention French and English, Beckett's range of quotations was vast. As already known, Italian literature in particular meant to Beckett first of all Dante, occasionally Petrarch or Pirandello; as to Leopardi, I think he can actually be recognised as probably the second major Italian influence on Beckett, after Dante.

Like Beckett, Leopardi linked his poetics and literary work with the deep reflections of a *philosophe*, whose European relevance is now being studied. The striking analogy of positions seems to suggest Leopardi's important influence on Beckett's criticism of the code he is exploring in *Endgame*, and a specific possible meaning in the outcome of the 'chess game' between Hamm and Clov.

Leopardi's Boy and Beckett's *Môme*

The mystery of the boy in the final scene of *Endgame*, interpreted by critics in completely different ways, can be considered as a major enigma in the play. The inexplicable difference between the original French version mentioning '*un môme*' with Moses' eyes, and the English version, by its very author and in which the scene has become shorter and no mention of Moses appears, simplifies the text but complicates the enigma. Beckett has in fact left both versions extant, and translations into other languages vary according to their derivation from either the French or the English edition. The German version, after its revision imposed in 1968 by Beckett on its translator, Elmar Tophoven, is based on the 'simplified' English version.

As James Knowlson pointed out, Beckett uses multiple quotation, while single quotation 'is anathema' to him.[10] In the French edition the boy with Moses' eyes can indeed refer to the Bible, but can also, as seen, lead back to *The Tempest* through the Clov/Caleb implications. As to Beckett's unusual association of a small boy with Moses dying—in old age according to the Bible—it can imply in its turn one more quotation, this time from Marcel Duchamp, to whom the play probably owes its title. In one of his works, *Obligation for the Monte Carlo Roulette*, Duchamp represented himself ironically as a shaven Moses and, according to Maurizio Calvesi, he probably imitated Albrecht Dürer's *Paedogeron*, a small boy with an old man's beard, in his *Gioconda* with whiskers.[11] Such material could well have suggested Beckett the double irony of 'shaving' Moses (usually shown as an old man with a long beard, as in Michelangelo's statue), and of turning the old man into a boy, as in the *Paedogeron*, that Beckett could see in Paris at the Louvre. Irony on alchemic implications—typical of Duchamp according to Calvesi—may well account for the added detail of the '*pierre levée*' the boy is leaning against in *Fin de partie*, which seems to hint at the alchemic 'child-Lapis' of natural eternal regeneration.

But by reducing the boy's passage in the English version, Beckett seems to have erased all such sources, as relevant for *Fin de partie* but less so for *Endgame*. Has he actually renounced the complexity of quotations in English, or has he favoured a different quotation, probably implied from the beginning along with the others, but left obscure by multiple superimposition? In fact in the same play Beckett often varies quotations according to the language: if the very 'our revels passage' from *The Tempest* is evident in *Endgame* only in the English version, also what has been recognised as a quotation from Baudelaire in the French version appears in the English text[12] as a double quotation from both Baudelaire and T. S. Eliot. Once left with no reference to Moses, what are the possible meanings of the *Endgame* boy in the English edition?

To the common reader it must obviously refer to nature and its capacity for generation, in spite of Hamm's and Clov's consensual definition of the outside world as a desert devoid of life, the more so as the boy looks at his own navel, the sign of birth. This indeed must be the primary meaning of the image within both the economy of the play and its philosophical implications.

In his 1930 essay on Proust, Beckett underlines in the French author's view on life (in which he mirrors his own outlook) a sharing with what he defines a kind of knowledge common to 'all wise thinkers', aiming not at the satisfaction of desires, but at their deletion, and the range of such thinkers is defined as 'from Brahma to Leopardi'. To confirm this attitude he then quotes, in the Italian original, lines 4 and 5 from Giacomo Leopardi's poem *A se stesso*:

> *In noi di cari inganni,*
> *Non che la speme, il desiderio è spento.*
>
> [Of our endeared delusions
> Hope is in us spent, as wishful desire with it]

As pointed out by John Barnes in an article on Leopardi's fortune in Ireland, stressing Beckett's interest for the Italian poet—probably dating from his third year at University in Dublin, when he studied Leopardi—the sources of Beckett's negative thought are many, including Geulincx and Schopenhauer in particular, but the fact that only Leopardi is here chosen to illustrate the point is obviously meaningful.[13]

Beckett, Barnes notes, does not quote Leopardi again as openly in later works, but more critics seem to have traced Leopardi's influence on Beckett's works, particularly in the insisted *acedia* of most of Beckett's 1937–39 poems and of many of his characters, such as Murphy, Watt[14] or Molloy. A fit inscription to *Malone Dies* could well be Leopardi's famous '*àl gener nostro il fato / non donò che il morire*' (once more from *À se stesso*), as Mr Robinson pointed out in his 1969 study on Beckett,[15] where another link between the two authors is found just in *Endgame*. Here Robinson connects the very setting of the play with one of Leopardi's *Operette morali* (Moral Pieces), *Il Cantico del gallo silvestre* (The Woodcock's Chant), quoting a specific passage:

> *Tempo verrá, che esso universo, e la natura medesima, sarà spenta. [. . .] del mondo intero, e delle infinite vicende e calamità delle cose create, non rimarrà pure un vestigio; ma un silenzio nudo, e una quiete altissima, empieranno lo spazio immenso. Così questo arcano mirabile e spaventoso dell'esistenza universale, innanzi di essere dichiarato nè inteso, si dileguerà e perderassi.* (Robinson, pp. 274–76)
>
> [The time will come when the universe and nature itself will be finished. [. . .] of the whole world and of the infinite vicissitudes

and adversities of created things not even a trace will remain; but naked silence and deepest quietude will fill infinite space. Thus this wondrous and fearsome mystery of universal existence, before ever being disveiled or penetrated, will dissolve and be lost.]

In Emanuele Severino's recent study of Giacomo Leopardi, *Il nulla e la poesia* (Nothingness and Poetry), the poet's thought—known and appreciated by Schopenhauer and Nietzsche as well—is seen as a forerunning turning point for the following century and for the contemporary philosophical and cultural main trend of western thought. Leopardi, Severino points out, was a *poet-philosophe*, and can be considered as a post-enlightenment nihilistic watershed in European thought, just as, we could add, Beckett is today considered a literary-philosophical watershed of postmodernism. According to Severino, indeed, Nietzsche in particular found in Leopardi a source more relevant than the opening reference to the Italian poet in his *Von Nutzen und Nachteil der Historie für das Leben* (About the Usefulness and Damage of History for Life), could in itself imply.[16] But most probably also Leopardi's influence on Beckett was more relevant than so far considered.

In 1835, in his *Palinodia*, Giacomo Leopardi gave a definition of nature as possible after the development of enlightenment or what he called 'the philosophy of disillusionment', summarising his thought ever since at least his *Dialogo della Natura e di un Islandese* (Dialogue of Nature with an Islander) in his *Operette morali*. In a long passage nature is here referred to as '*la natura crudel, fanciullo invitto*', cruel nature as an unvanquished boy, indifferent to man's destiny and his pretence at a central position in the universe, or 'anthropocentrism'. The image of nature as a boy is here suggested by Heraclitus' fragment 52, emphasising his capacity for playing endlessly at meaningless generation and destruction: in Leopardi's words, like a boy, nature '*il suo capriccio adempie, e senza posa distruggendo e formando si trastulla*', 'follows its whims and, restlessly destroying and generating, sports himself'.[17] Beckett's '*môme*' or boy in *Endgame* would indeed fit very well in the play if its meaning were partaking of Leopardi's nature as a '*fanciullo invitto*'. On the other hand many passages in Beckett's play recall passages not only from *Cantico del gallo silvestre* but from many of Leopardi's *Operette morali*, and their negative pervasive conception of nature.

This appears even more evident in the light of the previous preparatory versions of Beckett's play, especially in the two-act *Fin de partie* already quoted. Here Hamm and Clov discuss more at large than in the final text their relation to nature much as Leopardi's Islander poses questions to Nature itself, when he meets her in Africa. Clov's and Hamm's words imply Leopardi's very starting point, the centrality of man's relation to nature after the 'death of God', and a typical ironical step-mother image of nature itself, as the result of a negative development of the Utopian attitude of enlightenment. To Hamm and Clov nature means in fact the wastes of time in man's body and mind: 'We lose our hair, our teeth! Our bloom! Our ideals!'.

Moreover, Hamm's passion for the centre—Hamm insists on being placed right in the centre of his room—seems to dramatise one of Leopardi's most striking *Operette*: the *Dialogo di un folletto e di uno gnomo* (Dialogue of a Sprite and a Gnome) where man's anthropocentric pretension, his deep illusion of a 'natural right' to a central position in the world and nature, is ridiculed in a context of extinction of the human race, in a supposedly ended world: the very scene of *Endgame*.

Similarly, a long passage on the dead in *Waiting for Godot* recalls another of the *Operette morali*, the Dialogue of Federico Ruysch and his mummies: when Estragon and Vladimir evoke 'all the dead voices', that 'speak' in the natural noises of wings, or leaves or sand. Such voices 'whisper' or 'rustle' or 'murmur', because 'to have lived is not enough for them', and 'they have to talk about it', just like the mummies of Ruysch, that refuse to stay dead, and have to talk to Ruysch in analogous whisperings and murmurs. This similarity is actually completed in *Endgame*, in Hamm's and Clov's attitude towards death: to them the end means a quiet final passage to definite dissolution, just as in the mummies' description of their own deaths to Ruysch.

But with Leopardi Beckett seems to share also that 'poetics of objects' that S. Battaglia underlines in the Italian poet, who indeed insisted in his *Pensieri* (*Thoughts*) on the art of choosing the objects capable, in their very nature, to express or represent the artist's urge. In his opposition to romanticism, Leopardi seems to anticipate both Eliot's theory of the objective correlative and Beckett's use of objects or concrete forms. In this light the boy at the end of *Endgame*, if related to Leopardi's '*fanciullo invitto*', becomes a clear objectification of the two protagonists' relation to nature. He denounces the protagonists' specific *pseudos* on the world outside their refuge, while at the same time stating, in more general terms, the inextinguishable quality of nature at large implied in Leopardi's 'fanciullo invitto'. In Leopardi's terms the boy means nature's becoming, endless and 'evergreen', as contrasted with the single individual's destiny of destruction.

According to Severino, Leopardi's 'fanciullo invitto' mirrors—much earlier than Nietzsche—an anticipated 'discovery' of Heraclitus and presocratic thought, the source of a double definition of nature: as determined forms of being, individuals or specific worlds, damned to end; and as *kosmos*, or undetermined, continual becoming, eternal duration, as defined in Heraclitus' fragment 30. Leopardi's own comment on the passage that closes his *Woodcock's Chant* (the last of the *Operette*), quoted above, is indeed that the end of the world envisaged there is 'a poetical conclusion', but not 'a philosophical one': philosophically speaking, 'being, that never began, will never end', '*parlando filosoficamente, l'esistenza che non è mai cominciata, non avrà mai fine*' (see G. Leopardi, *Opere*, ed. S. Solmi, Ricciardi, Milano 1956, pp. 677–78). It can be in this sense that *Endgame* starts with the meaningful 'finished, it's finished, nearly finished, it must be nearly finished', where the end is at the same time real and certain, unreal and impossible.

By leaving out in *Endgame* the reference to Moses present in *Fin de partie*, Beckett's boy, no longer biblical or 'alchemic', seems to stand out literally as Leopardi's '*nuda natura*', watching his own navel, or law of reproduction, at the same time indifferent to the destiny of the individual, who in turn breaks his link with nature by denying its manifestations. The philosophical implications, reducing life to nothingness, to Nature's accidental coming out of and going back to nothingness—also implicit in Hamm's story on the father whose child he did not help nourish because life is helpless—are here close to Leopardi's positions, not hindered by the more complex range of allusions in French.

For Leopardi, who must according to S. Timpanaro be considered thoroughly within the tradition of enlightenment,[18] philosophy has by his age become '*scelleraggine ragionata*',[19] reasonable criminality: it must indeed accept immoral egoism as the outcome of a meaningless world dominated by unavoidable suffering and death, frustrating the individual's natural desire for pleasure.

Heir to d'Holbach's materialism, as well as to Voltaire's or Rousseau's thought, Leopardi—writing in the tradition of the *philosophe*—theorises the role of the poet-philosopher, and both his poetry and his *Thoughts* mirror the same central conception of nature as negative. Man is considered only within nature and nature appears '*matrigna*', a stepmother to him, disattending his anthropocentric illusions, taking no care of his griefs and suffering. The poet-philosopher's task must then be twofold: a clearcut awareness of such a condition, a full intellectual consciousness and, on the other hand, a capacity to develop what he calls an *ultra-filosofia*,[20] a 'philosophy of resistance', able to partly recover the illusions to be used by the individual while waiting for his end. The first task corresponds to Beckett's *dianoia*, to his determination to know man's real condition and read his deprivation of sense as the consequence of a relentless analysis. Leopardi's second task instead is less considered by Beckett, although he accepts Leopardi's capacity for obstinate resistance. But this task is, in a more complex way, at the very centre of the postmodern outlook.

In his last poem *La ginestra, il fiore del deserto* (The Broom Plant, Desert Flower, 1837), Leopardi praises the broom plant growing in the volcanic desert produced by Vesuvius as the only one able to survive in such an environment, ready to ply to the violence of the volcano and to start again after destruction. Here, more than ever in Leopardi's poetry, is a form of the sublime, expressing resistance to death and the thought of its proximity. Solidarity among men against destroying nature, '*la social catena* [. . .] *contro l'empia natura*', enforced by 'justice and pity', '*giustizia e pietade*' (*Palinodia*, vv. 148–53), are then suggested as the main values left.

Beckett's sublime is analogous to Leopardi's, capable of transcending in the mind the terrors of nature, of facing all the grief of life through poetry; and pity, the pity that ties Clov to Hamm and allows him no real escape from their refuge, expresses what is left of Leopardi's solidarity enhanced in *La ginestra*. In *Not I* Beckett was to link the problem of pity with that of justice in the protagonist's memory of being questioned at courts whether guilty or not.

Yet Beckett has no real equivalent to Leopardi's broom plant, his sense of resistance being rather envisaged by Hamm's melancholia as by the melancholia of the protagonist of Beckett's last piece, Walther von der Vogelweide, a character actually already evoked in one of the early versions of *Fin de partie*.[21] Walther sitting on a rock while thinking of the moral and philosophical paradoxes in man's life, allows no rebuilding of illusions. In this sense Beckett's awareness of inescapable grief is a sterner one, while at the same time delving deeper into the individual, far beyond Leopardi's 'theory of pleasure'. If this theory is based on the central natural paradox of the opposition between the destruction of natural change and the individual's as natural infinite thirst for pleasure and narcissism, admitting of no death or illness, Beckett's theory of 'funny unhappiness' reaches deep into the unconscious. In a sense Hamm—who is proud of his suffering and of the suffering he imposes on Clov—is an evolution of Leopardi's trauma, that stops short of Leopardi's task of recovering illusion, but delves farther into gnoseological problems. In *Endgame* illusions have been destroyed from the very beginning, but the reasons for the destruction are finally questioned and 'delegitimated': the negative, 'absurd' outcome of the code of enlightenment developed by Leopardi has come full circle in Beckett, but has also reached its 'bursting point'.

Walther's Post Paradox

As much a poet-philosopher as Leopardi, Beckett ends his work with the image of Walther on his rock and its paradoxical implications. While Leopardi despairs of the Utopian tradition typical of enlightenment, Beckett implies a further step: he reaches a point where *any* description of the external world is made senseless by internal drives, this way opening to postmodern hermeneutics.

The difference between Leopardi and Beckett is marked by an impediment, an '*empêchement*' theorised by Beckett, that precludes the object to the perception, and hinders the subject's attempts at the representation of the object, or even of the subject to himself.[22]

For Leopardi reality is the brutal indifference of nature, the careless generation of creatures and the ultimate lack of control of the creatures over their own destiny. For Beckett reality is a necessarily unfaithful representation, a distorted choice, a problem of knowledge beyond Leopardi's reach. By destroying illusions, Leopardi had destroyed man's *récits* on the world, reaching the farthest point allowed within the desemiotisation of enlightenment; but by destroying representation itself Beckett has finally no subject and no reality to vindicate. If Leopardi's creature is motherless, Beckett's is also speechless, as in *Not I*; or in turn uselessly talking too much, trying to fill up the void of impossible representation with vain words.

Beckett's '*fanciullo invitto*' in *Endgame* is not only an irrision at the individual's pretences, he finally 'falsifies' Hamm's and Clov's interaction and unnecessary, although inescapable, sufferings. If for Leopardi '*il fanciullo invitto*' defeated the individual's expectancies of his centrality in the world, in Beckett's theatre, where the centre is still keenly looked after as in Hamm's case, awareness has gone so far as to disintegrate the inner centrality of the I within himself. Rather than fighting against external dangers, the individual must now fight against internal self-destruction, against a trend to catatonia, an inner paralysis that turns the whole world into putrefaction and death, in comparison with which, ironically, the '*fanciullo invitto*' now becomes an assessment of life, that gives the life to Hamm's and Clov's outlook.

A beyond is thus paradoxically opened up through the very extremity of a code of destruction, virtually redisclosing the 'narrative capacity' of the other codes, of the illusions they have given birth to in the past, now as equally illusory as the outcome of the radical criticism enacted. The self-criticism of the code of enlightenment can indeed open up to all other codes, no longer as Truth, but as a range of relative possibilities as illusory as their negation. Leopardi's *ultra-filosofia* of a conscious use of illusions, that Beckett does not seem to consider, inevitably becomes the next step, the beyond: not as a moral or psychological device, but as an epistemological necessity in a different view.

By 'adding' Beckett to Leopardi and Leopardi to Beckett, the process of contemporary culture leading to postmodernism—Beckett's immediate beyond—becomes clearer, while even the definition of postmodernism can acquire a new semiotic sense and explanation, as the product of the end of that dominance of one of the main codes Lotman describes as typical, so far, of western civilisation. Using Juri Lotman's semiotic terms, postmodernism can indeed be seen as the limitless but potentially creative, conscious opening up of the full range of the relative encoding possibilities of the human mind, made possible by the end of the dominance of one code, and calling for a new difficult responsibility of choice.

Beckett stops before such a landscape, he himself has helped prepare by erasing preceding landscapes, while Leopardi would never have dared to think in terms of such a wide *ultra-filosofia*, the possibility of which he had nevertheless theorised.

Notes

1. Giuseppina Restivo, 'La Waste Land di Eliot, il deserto di Beckett', in *Il confronta letterario*, No. 4 (1985).

2. See P. Watzlawick, J. H. Beavin, D. Jackson, *Pragmatic of Human Communication*, New York, 1967, and Cesare Segre, who in *La funzione del linguaggio nell'*Acte sans paroles *di S. Beckett* (in *Le strutture e il tempo* (Turin: Einaudi 1974) analyses Beckett's theatre in terms of the above mentioned theory of the double bind.

3. Didier Anzieu, *L'autoanalyse de Freud* (Paris: PUF 1975). This relationship and its influence on *Endgame* is enlarged on in G. Restivo, *Le soglie del postmoderno: 'Finale di partita'* (*The Postmodern watershed: Endgame*), Il Mulino, Bologna (in press).

4. The play of the cultural codes in *The Tempest* is discussed in G. Restivo, 'Ironie anticlassiche nella "Tempesta" di Shakespeare' in *Il confronto letterario*, No. 1 (1984).

5. See Enoch Brater, 'Noah, Not I and Beckett's Incomprehensible Sublime' in *Comparative Drama*, Fall 1974, No. 3, and G. Restivo, *Le soglie del postmoderno*, cit.

6. Roger Toumson, *Trois Calibans* (Havana: Edición Casa de las Américas ciudad de la Habana 1981).

7. See *Fin de partie*, Typescript 1, preserved in the Ohio State University Library, p.25.

8. See Juri Lotman, 'Il problema del segno e del sistema segnico nella tipologia della cultura russa prima del XX secolo', in Lotman and Uspenskij eds., *Ricerche semiotiche, Nuove tendenze delle scienze umane nell'URSS* (Turin: Einaudi 1973).

9. In an early version of *Fin de partie*, in Hamm's final monologue two of the three key words of the French revolution—*égalité* and *fraternité*—are meaningfully introduced, and one of them—*égalité*—remains in the final French edition.

10. James Knowlson, 'Beckett's Bits of Pipe', in *Samuel Beckett: Humanistic Perspectives*, ed. S. E. Gontarski (Ohio State UP 1983).

11. Maurizio Calvesi, *Duchamp invisibile* (Rome: Officina edizioni 1975).

12. See 'La Waste Land di Eliot, il deserto di Beckett', cit.

13. See John C. Barnes, 'La fortuna di Leopardi in Irlanda', in the Acts of the Leuven conference on Leopardi on December 10–12, 1987, printed in Musarra, Vanvolsem, Guglielmone Lamberti, *Leopardi e la cultura europea* (Rome: Bulzoni 1989; also printed in English by Leuven UP).

14. John Pilling, *Samuel Beckett* (London: Routledge & Kegan Paul 1976), p. 61.

15. Michael Robinson, *The Long Sonata of the Dead: A Study of Samuel Beckett* (London: Hart-Davis 1969), pp. 163–4, 312.

16. Emanuele Severino, *Il nulla e la poesia* (Milan: Rizzoli 1990), p.20.

17. Giacomo Leopardi, *Palinodia*, vv. 171–2.

18. Salvatore Timpanaro, *Classicismo e illuminismo nell'Ottocento italiano*, Nistri-Lischi, Pisa, 1965, p.40. The *Introduction* and the chapter 'Alcune osservazioni sul pensiero di Leopardi' amply prove and insist on Leopardi's ascendancies within the tradition of enlightenment.

19. *Pensieri.*

20. Ibid.

21. In the Ohio Typescript mentioned above, Hamm's father is called P, but also occasionally Walther.

22. 'Peintres de l'empêchement' (Paris: Cahiers de l'Herne 1976), p. 67.

LOIS GORDON

The Language of Dreams: The Anatomy of the Conglomerative Effect

"Play" [is the] natural activity of all living things (human animal), and its goal is beyond "self-preservation"; it is a way of removing the "burden" of human existence as it "deepens" our connection with ourselves. If the dream functions for the same purpose—as relief and continuity, one might suggest that *the dream* is all we have in our desperation; it is the modern equivalent of religion—a new (another) form of play, a form of relief without transcendence, without mysticism, our only would-be, not greatly successful, escape from pain.

—Hans-Georg Gadamer

Dream thoughts . . . cannot . . . have any definite endings; they are bound to branch out in every direction into the intricate network of our world of thought.

—Sigmund Freud

We have discussed dreams as absurd, but examples have taught us how sensible a dream can be even when it appears to be absurd.

—Sigmund Freud

Having considered secondary revision and the conglomerative meaning of *Godot,* I can turn to the bizarre, illogical fragments and dialogue exchanges that compose a major part of the play. The dense, cryptic, contradictory nature of this material is accomplished by specific rhetorical devices akin to those described in *The Interpretation of Dreams.* The following includes examples of displacement, condensation, plastic pictorialization, and multiple manifestations of paralogic, all of which reject causation and temporal linearity. If, to Freud, intrapsychic mechanisms allow the individual disguised outlets (dreams) in which to express repressed (ego-censored) feelings, for Beckett they become unique poetic techniques with which to elaborate the conglomerate *emotional* experience—in *Godot*, the feeling of precarious survival in the incohesive worlds of self and the universe.

Freud described the dreamer as a poet but hastened to add that the final dream scenario would always remain unedited, a drama derived from an entirely personal vocabulary, and that final interpretation would be inconclusive. In addition, given the transformational energy propelling dreams, one could always anticipate a sense of excitement from the dream and an evocation of infinite meaning only rarely equaled in the theater.[1] Dreams are, after all, continuously innovative and improvisational, and since they are the creation of the dreamer they are never boring. Finally, these translations of psychic energy always generate wonder (Freud's word) from their unique construction upon vertical and horizontal spatial and temporal axes that reflect the continuously evolving and metamorphosing energy beneath dream transformations, as well as those elements of rational thought against which unconscious revelations continuously vibrate. All the same, to Freud, underlying, alinear patterns might allow one to decipher partial meanings, in addition to the conglomerative effect. In fact, one can be quite specific in outlining how the recurrence of certain patterns described by Freudian analysts as typical of dream or unconscious thought[2] provides what they call the grammar of *Godot*.

One might begin at any point in the play and trace transformational patterns via a variety of avenues: the unique rhythms of syntax and asymmetries of word association, the acoustical properties of words and their visual-verbal resemblances (homonyms), connotations acquired through alliteration, consonance and rhyming possibilities, the reversal of parts of speech, as well as metonymy, synecdoche, synesthesia, puns, personification, and oxymoron. For example, in *Godot* causal relations are obliterated, inverted, or set into contradiction. Estragon says, "Don't touch me! Don't question me! Don't speak to me! Stay with me!" Objects and events transform into one another: chicken bones become fish bones; night instantly transforms into day. The use of alternatives like either-or is similarly abandoned, with the result that both elements of disjunction are placed in a single context; in other words, either-or becomes both-and. As Beckett once said of him, Pozzo might be (a) Godot: he provides direction to Lucky and is mistaken for Godot when he appears.[3] Pozzo and Lucky, in addition, are at one and the same time master and slave to each other; Didi and Gogo's role reversals, discussed below, permit each to appear as the dependent, wise, or controlling figure.

The word *if*, which in logical thinking indicates wish or the conditional, is represented by simultaneity. In fact, the traditional logic implied in the use of conjunctions is entirely revised in unconscious thought process: *and*, *or*, *but*, *because*, *just as*, and *though* as well as *if* and *either-or* are indicated by simultaneity.[4] The need for a Godot is transformed into the belief that a meeting with him is imminent. All relations of similarity, correspondence, and contiguity are unified. Disjunctures of ordinary logic, time, and space, along with the absence of the conditional tense, result in the equation of the fantastic with the realistic. To Vladimir and Estragon, God is a businessman, consulting his family, friends, and bank accounts. It follows that when Pozzo appears before Vladimir and Estragon and is served his private communion of food and wine, he is mistaken for Godot. He presents himself as a successful entrepreneur who enjoys being treated, as he puts it, with "fear and trembling."

If the chain of these concretizations seems unending, so is the network of characters created from the aural and visual similarity of words (G*o*d*o*t/P*ozzo*/G*o*g*o*; Luck*y*/Did*i*; f*oo*t/b*oo*t); and from their bisyllabic (Didi/Gogo/Pozzo/Lucky) and trisyllabic pairings (Estragon/Vladimir), as well as pairings based on identical multiples from the alphabet: Estragon and Vladimir, consisting of eight letters; Pozzo/Lucky, five; Didi/Gogo, four; even more subtle is the construction of *D*idi's and *G*ogo's names after those of the two hanged thieves, *D*ysmas and *G*estas. (Beckett's pair frequently ponder the mystery of salvation and damnation.)

Dream images and characters, like unconscious thought, are also formulated upon the literal, foreign, and etymological roots of words. Didi, from *dire*, to speak, is the partner who contemplates and prefers that Lucky "think"; Gogo (to go), Didi's opposite, is more physical and sensual, and he would have Lucky "dance." Each, regardless of his role or role reversal, concretely represents some dimension or playing out of the conglomerative effect. If Pozzo, in Italian, means "well" or "hole," his name concretizes the pun and paradox of whole and hole, completeness and emptiness, another manifestation of the circular and paradoxically imperative but useless waiting in the play. The condensations of *Lucky* are similarly rich, with Lucky (1) apparently lucky in having his Godot in Pozzo, (2) illustrating the ambiguity and gratuitousness of luck, as Pozzo puts it, "I might just as well have been in his shoes and he mine. If chance had willed otherwise," (3) representing a modern-day Luke, patron saint of artists who wrote of the two thieves and also said, as Beckett ultimately implies, "The Kingdom of God(ot) is within you" (17:21). Luke is also iconographically associated with the calf, which is gastronomically associated with tarragon (in French, *estragon*). (4) Lucky is "raised" by Estragon and Vladimir in act I and is related to yet another biblical figure, Lazarus. The list is endless—for another example, as a mad dancer, Lucky suggests Joyce's daughter, Lucia, also mad and a dancer.

Dream concretizations extend to the imprecise use of words and temporal dislocations: "Once in a way [not "while"]" and "Getup till I embrace you" (act I) and "Come here till I embrace you [not "so that I can"]" (act II)—and their simultaneously oppositional meanings. Lucky dances "The Net," which, like the rock (Peter's church/Cain's weapon in slaying Abel) and tree (the Garden of Eden/site of the Crucifixion), elicits multiple associations with emptiness and redemption (for example, captivity and rescue). These condensations enrich the sparse dialogue and setting with multiple levels of meaning.

A word may be repeated or used simultaneously as different parts of speech, once again reinforcing the conglomerative effect. When the four major characters fall, Beckett uses *fall* as both a noun and verb, and the figures fall down upon one another in the shape of a cross; at one time, the four form a double cruciform. The same holds true of their lifting up or raising of Pozzo and Lucky. As Beckett directed, when Lucky is uplifted, he is to stand between Vladimir and Estragon with outstretched arms, in another configuration of the cross.

Waiting, Vladimir and Estragon's paradoxical life activity, is repeated not just in the "Let's go. (*They do not move.*)" refrain but in subtle repetitions of the word *again*, generating both a sense of stasis and movement: "*Estragon gives up, exhausted, rests, tries again*" and Vladimir's "There you are again . . . There we are again . . . There I am again." Waiting, like the phrase "Nothing to be done," is concretely played out in many activities and verbal interchanges, such as in Vladimir and Estragon's waiting for Lucky to dance and for night to fall and in their repeated statements "Nothing happens," "Nobody comes, nobody goes, it's awful," and "What do we do now?" Beckett listed 109 instances of waiting in one Production Notebook, each an intended variation of the larger waiting for Godot.[5]

Vladimir's song at the beginning of act II generates its own sense of infinite regression or waiting—for a denouement. Repeating, without conclusion, the tale of a dog beaten to death by a cook, after which several dogs bury the dead, after which the dog is beaten to death, after which several dogs bury the dead . . . is another example of oblivion and gratuitous benevolence, another example of the conglomerative effect: a tale waiting for a conclusion. It is also a fitting introduction to a second act that repeats and elaborates upon this subject.

To return to the brief distinctions made in chapter 3 between dream or unconscious thought (primary process) and rational thought (secondary process), I want to explain the paralogic of primary process, which has its own unique rules of structure. In addition to being personalized, rather than goal directed, and often perceived as gibberish or nonsense, it is typified by non sequiturs, for it is not bound by the everyday usage of time and space. In addition, whereas in logical, secondary process, the subject of a minor premise is always included in the major one (for example, in All men are mortal. Socrates is a man . . . , "Socrates" is part of "all men"), in primary process paralogic, the subject of the minor premise is *never* included in the subject of the major one. For example, in Certain Indians are swift. Stags are swift, and so on, one would not rationally conclude that all stags are Indians. But in paralogic, objects may be equated on the basis of a single property, here, the common swiftness of stags and certain Indians.[6] In *Godot*, when Pozzo announces, "I am blind," Estragon paralogically connects blindness with Tiresias and then says of Pozzo, "Perhaps he can see into the future," as though all blind men were prophets. using the same kind of paralogic, Lucky says he is a poet because he wears rags. A more elaborate illustration and example of condensation is Vladimir's reply to Estragon's suggestion that they hang themselves. "Hmmm," he begins. "It'd [suicide] give us an erection." While it may be true that hanging causes this physiological reaction, Vladimir's subsequent remarks reinforce the entirely paralogical nature of his thoughts: "With all that follows. Where it falls mandrakes grow. That's why they shriek when you pull them up. Did you not know that?" Mandrakes may have physical similarities with the human body, and shrieking and dying may, at least poetically, be associated with both the sexual act and the sound of the plant when it is uprooted, but Vladimir and Estragon are not plants, and the main issue under discussion is not sexual. Vladimir is unable or unwilling to rationally consider their suicide. The closest he gets to it, pursuing his paralogical thought further, is in his association of death, or the body's hanging, and the Fall. He says, "Where it falls mandrakes grow", but his "it" would seem to refer to his erection. To both Vladimir and Estragon, hanging is associated with the Fall, the result of the (original) sin of simply being born. Vladimir paralogically equates the visual similarity of an erection with hanging, along with his other associations of death, shrieking, and sexual response.

An even more intricate example of paralogic and condensation that highlights the complexities and contradictions of the conglomerative effect occurs in Vladimir's "Hope deferred maketh the something sick," a rewording of Proverbs 13:12, "Hope deferred maketh the heart sick: but when the desire cometh, it is a tree of life." Vladimir takes the first half of the statement concretely and concludes that postponing hope, that is, waiting for Godot, makes, so to speak, a vague "something" ill. The proverb rests on a belief in the future ("but when"): if one defers hope, one's heart aches, but when one regains faith (the "desire" to hope), one is reinvigorated or resurrected. Vladimir's collapsing of the conditional "but when" into a flat, declarative statement, "Hope maketh the something sick," militates against the option of change. Time or chronology, specifically, future redemption ("but when"), has been deleted.

"The something sick" restates the conglomerative effect that humankind "wastes and pines": Vladimir's pained loins, Estragon's feet, Pozzo's heart, lungs, and blindness, and Lucky's running sore and mute condition. But Vladimir's omission of "desire" in his remark may be a totally personal statement—genital problems trouble him throughout the play—and may echo the absence of physical or spiritual passion in the play. His omission of "desire" may reinforce the (heart)sickness brought on by his physical/spiritual condition. The play as a whole becomes a working out of hope deferred versus hope retained, the wavering resolve to await Godot and the heartsickness that that brings.

When Vladimir says, "What's the use of losing heart now? We should have thought of it a million years ago, in the nineties," he distorts time. He juxtaposes what might be called figurative language or slang, "losing heart" and "a million years ago," with a concrete date, "in the nineties". Again, when Estragon answers Vladimir regarding how long he has been unhappy, his eccentric use of verb tense in "I'd [not "I've"] forgotten" dislocates chronology, which allows him to gain some distance from the truth of his present predicament.

Dislocations, distortions, and misunderstandings of time fill the play: "The light suddenly fails [not falls]" and "In a moment it is night"; "It must be Spring. / But in a single night!" In answer to the question "Is it evening?" the following exchange occurs:

> *Silence. Vladimir and Estragon scrutinize the sunset.*
> ESTRAGON: It's rising.
> VLADIMIR: Impossible.
> ESTRAGON: Perhaps it's dawn.

Each of these examples demonstrates the asyndetic omission of causal links or logical connections that traditionally focus a statement toward a goal.[7] Although sections of Lucky's monologue exemplify asyndetic non sequiturs as well as paradox and concretizations ("[God] loves us dearly with some exceptions for reasons unknown but time will tell"), asyndetic omissions recur within seemingly comprehensible interchanges. When Estragon is asked if he remembers the holy lands, he replies, "I remember the maps of the Holy Lands. Coloured they were. Very pretty. The Dead Sea was pale blue. The very look of it made me thirsty. That's where we'll go . . . for our honeymoon." Although the comment may reflect Estragon's childlike sensory pleasures or his deep-seated hostility to Vladimir (discussed below), one's first response is that his reply is not focused on answering Vladimir's question. Again, the personalized response avoids the question. Estragon connects the memory of a color with past thirst and suggests, for the future, that they go to the traditional source of spiritual succor (the Holy Lands). Estragon is always aware of his fallen state.

Asyndetic thinking frequently has a poetic quality, although it is a poetry born of an entirely personal idiom. Words, independent of consensual associational meaning, become affective, like the rhythmical or rhyming sounds of a foreign language, as in Lucky's "Feckham, Peckham, Fulham, Clapham" and Estragon's "Macon" and "Cackon". Using approximations or "substitute words" is also poetic but, again, meaning remains private. Pozzo, who has difficulty breathing, says, "I can't find my pulverizer," when he means *vaporizer.*

Words that lack referentiality and are askewed from a logical goal often lend the dialogue an autistic quality: for example, when Vladimir says to Estragon, "Calm yourself," he replies, "Calm . . . calm . . . The English say cawm, . . . You know the story of the Englishman in the brothel?" The concretized anecdote that follows may (1) allow Estragon a story appropriate to his own hedonistic interests, (2) provoke Vladimir by alluding to his problematic genital ailment, (3) comfort Vladimir by distracting him with a joke or pun, or (4) allow the two, after their temporary crisis, to return to their set role playing. Although Estragon's story may serve one, all, or none of these functions, the only certainty is that it makes no clear, goal-directed sense.

"Clang associations" typify asyndetic poetic dialogue, uniting words on the basis of their common vowel or consonantal sounds. The following exchange illustrates how each speaker imbues his words with an entirely personal meaning. Estragon has mistaken Pozzo for Godot:

> ESTRAGON: Bozzo . . . Bozzo . . .
> VLADIMIR: Pozzo . . . Pozzo . . .
> ESTRAGON: PPPOZZZO!
> VLADIMIR: Is it Pozzo or Bozzo?
> ESTRAGON: Pozzo . . . no. . . . I'm afraid I . . . no . . . I don't seem to. . . . . .
> VLADIMIR: I once knew a family named Gozzo.

A kind of primitive poetry fills the play in its many sequences of repeated dialogue:

> POZZO: What was I saying? . . . What was I saying?
> ESTRAGON: What'll we do, what'll we do.

and

VLADIMIR: The tree!
ESTRAGON: The tree!

and

VLADIMIR: It'd give us an erection!
ESTRAGON: . . . An erection!

So, too, Lucky's definition of God's "apathia . . . athambia . . . aphasia" describes the limitations of God's powers, as well as the gratuitousness of His benevolence. But his stringing together of words, as in "running cycling swimming flying floating riding gliding conating," may be motivated more by the sounds of the words and their rhythmical properties than by his intent to state that games or sports, like every other human activity, lead to oblivion.

The foregoing accounts for how proper names in dreams may be generated through aural, visual, or phonetic similarities. Some, like Godot/Pozzo, deserve additional attention because they take unto themselves paralogical and, at times, magical thinking. Pozzo, "made in God's image," enjoys being regarded with "fear and trembling." Pozzo calls his underling Lucky Atlas, the son of Jupiter, and Estragon mistakes Pozzo for Godot, not only because he looks like their imagined Godot, but also because the *o* sound unites Pozzo, Godot, and Gogo in his mind. Furthermore, the *o* sound and the shape of a well, *pozzo* in Italian, function as emblems of totality and nothingness—the conglomerative meaning of waiting and game playing, reason and unreason, the circularity of wish, as opposed to the actuality of Godot. Finally, the *o* sound, as mentioned earlier, represents Bion's goal of psychic wholeness.

Magical thinking is exemplified in the use of synonyms and the incremental modification of proper names. As words or objects are endowed with magical qualities, Pozzo's search for his pipe ("briar") transforms into a perhaps more hopeful search for a "dudeen," which becomes his desperate quest for his "Kapp and Peterson," at which point he is "on the verge of tears." Estragon and Vladimir's urgency to return to their set repartee functions as a guarantee against ill fortune:

VLADIMIR: Say something!
ESTRAGON: I'm trying!
VLADIMIR (*in anguish*): Say anything at all!

Beckett's logic would seem to be that game playing is, after all, ritual, and when ritual is invested with magical meaning, it becomes religion.

Concrete thinking, at the heart of primary process thought, has various manifestations in what are traditionally called abstraction or metaphoric equivalents, although the spatial gap (Jakobson's distinction between vertical and horizontal dimensions) is dissolved between the two parts of the analogy or metaphor. That is, the subtle distinction maintained in the use of *like* rather than *as* evaporates. Lucky is not a man who behaves like a beast of burden; he feels and is treated like an animal and is thus portrayed as one, complete with rope and a load to cart. Similarly, because Estragon is told that he and Vladimir are no longer tied to Godot, Estragon mistakes Pozzo for Godot simply because Pozzo holds Lucky on a rope. When asked if Vladimir is sixty or seventy, Estragon replies that he is eleven. Pozzo has great difficulty sitting because he concretizes standing as gaining (godlike or lunar) power: "How am I to sit down . . . now that I have risen?"

Because the unconscious is incapable of abstraction, primary process often transforms statements into pseudoabstractions or partially concretizes or distorts them completely. Estragon appears to understand Vladimir's "Let wait till we know exactly how we stand," but he fails to grasp Vladimir's next, contradictory statement: "Let's strike while the iron is hot." Estragon translates the metaphor concretely, first agreeing with Vladimir's initial statement that they wait, but then replying, "It might be better to strike the iron before it freezes." The sensual partner, who can never know how they stand (and who frequently totters), lacks any comprehension of the metaphor "Strike while the iron is hot." He says that it might therefore be better to act not by modifying their behavior in some undefined way, as Vladimir suggests, but by literally attacking the iron when, reversing Vladimir's sensory terms, the iron is cold but not yet frozen.

One of the most obvious examples of concrete thinking involves Vladimir and Estragon's relationship to Godot, a linking in which their wish is transformed into the certainty of their appointment. While in waking life it is mad to consider God in flesh-and-blood terms because God is a delusion as far as the senses tell us, in dreams, fears and hopes are enacted concretely, and one can thus expect Godot to be not like a father but, in fact, the father. As primary process articulates what secondary process analogizes, Vladimir and Estragon concretize the anthropomorphic deity as an actual flesh-and-blood person, Mr. Godot, a businessman:

ESTRAGON: What exactly did we ask [Godot] for? . . .
A vague supplication. . . . And what did he reply?
VLADIMIR:NThat he'd have to think it over.

ESTRAGON: In the quiet of his home.
VLADIMIR: Consult his family.
ESTRAGON: His friends.
VLADIMIR: His agents.
ESTRAGON: His correspondents.
VLADIMIR: His books.
ESTRAGON: His bank account.

Yet like the traditional godhead, their Godot requires "supplication," and at one point they say that if they abandoned or "dropped" Godot, "he'd punish us."

That all of the characters suffer from somatic complaints is another manifestation of concrete thinking, as it simultaneously conveys their metaphysical condition.[8] Vladimir and Estragon, for example, project their psychological and metaphysical pain onto, fittingly, a boot ("Go-go") and hat (for the thinker, Didi). Another example of primary process's concretization of abstraction involves the dramatic transformation of Pozzo and Lucky. Assured of his direction in life and confident of his control over time, Pozzo, in the daytime, in the sun, has literal vision. But nighttime frightens him. At one point he advises Vladimir and Estragon, "I'd wait till it was black night before I gave up." Elsewhere, Estragon says of Pozzo's fear, "Everything seems black to him to-day." It is thus concretely appropriate that at his "recognition scene," when humbled and aware of his meaningless and arrogant endeavors, he experiences his dark night of the soul and concretely becomes blind.

In the concretizing of abstractions, objects or metaphors are treated as though they were literally the things they may be said to represent: for example, Lucky's putting on his hat before he philosophizes, as though it were literally his "thinking hat"; Pozzo's remarking that Lucky "can't think without his hat"; Vladimir's comment after locating Lucky's hat: "Now our troubles are over"; Vladimir's earliest efforts to gain control over his life as "he takes off his hat, peers into it . . . [and] knocks on the crown"; and one of the play's funniest scenes, the vaudeville routine in which all the confused characters rapidly switch hats. Sometimes these objects become highly personalized. Not only do Vladimir and Pozzo read the sky and light as though it will personally announce their fate, that is, when Godot will come, but the sun and moon come to function like physical extensions of their minds and bodies.

If, existentially, the individual is the measure of his universe—author, actor, and director—unconsciously, one occupies that center concretely as both subject and object. Thus speaking in both the objective and nominative case, Estragon is, on the one hand, affected by the moon, for when it rises it "shed[s] a pale light on the scene"; on the other hand, he says *he* is "pale for weariness . . . of climbing and gazing on the likes of us." One of the play's most moving sequences involving the personalization of time occurs when Vladimir and Estragon have the illusion Godot has arrived and their eternal waiting has ceased. For them, tomorrow has come at last: "We are no longer alone, waiting for the night, . . . waiting for . . . waiting. . . . All evening we have struggled, unassisted. Now it's over. It's already tomorrow."

At one point, Estragon is the only character who knows that the true measurement of time is internal. He correctly contradicts Pozzo's "I hear nothing" with "I hear something," and he does this by listening to Pozzo's heart. At the other extreme, when Pozzo believed he could control time, he took comfort in his "half-hunter," which he admitted was an instrument of "deadbeat escapement." By act II, however, Pozzo's blindness, like Lucky's bags filled with detritus—mementos of meaninglessness—has become an emblem of human evanescence.

Notes

Note to epigraphs. Unless otherwise noted, all references to Freud's *Interpretation of Dreams* are cited from the Avon edition (New York, 1998); for these two epigraphs, see 564, 629. Continuing his discussion of the "absurd" in dreams, Freud wrote, 480, that dreams "are most often most profound when they seem most crazy. In every epoch of history those who have had something to say but could not say it without peril have eagerly assumed a fool's cap. The audience at whom their forbidden speech was aimed tolerated it more easily if they could at the same time laugh and flatter themselves with the reflection that the unwelcome words were clearly nonsensical."

1. Salomon Resnik, *The Theatre of the Dream*, trans. Alan Sheridan (London: Tavistock Publishers, 1987), 17–19. Resnik relates Freud's dream theory to a number of contemporary philosophers often connected with Beckett and, of particular interest, with psychoanalysts associated with the Tavistock, including W. R. D. Fairbairn, Melanie Klein, D. W. Winnicott, as well as Bion. Throughout *The Interpretation of Dreams*, Freud speaks of dreams as "dramatizations" of ideas, often using the word *absurd* to define the "mood of the dream thoughts, which combines derision or laughter with contradiction." See 470, 86–87, 65–67, 97. See also David Foulkes, *Grammar of Dreams* (New York: Basic Books, 1978), and Bert O. States, *The Rhetoric of Dreams* (Ithaca: Cornell University Press, 1988), and *Seeing in the Dark: Reflections on Dreams and Dreaming* (New Haven: Yale University Press, 1997). States has written a number of outstanding books on dreams as well as one about *Waiting for Godot* in which he does not discuss dreams: *The Shape of Paradox* (Berkeley: University of California Press, 1978). In *Seeing in the Dark*, he writes, "Dreaming and art-making . . . share a 'technique' of purification of waking experience. They are essentializing processes, as aestheticians say. [They ask] you to look at things you haven't been seeing" (6–7).

2. Although this information appears to be commonplace among psychiatrists and psychologists, the following will introduce the nonspecialist to generally accepted theories about unconscious functioning and the rhetorical devices that

characterize dreams, Freud's "royal road to the unconscious." In addition to *The Interpretation of Dreams*, see Freud's "Neurosis and Psychosis" and "The Loss of Reality in Neurosis and Psychosis," *General Psychological Theory*, trans. Joan Riviere (New York: Collier, 1963), 185–89, and 202–6, respectively. See also note 9, chap. 3. For quick reference to Freud's definitions of the components of the dream (which he frequently compares to a picture puzzle, or "rebus"), see, in *The Interpretation of Dreams*, his discussion of condensation (a "bizarre composite image or word"), 212, 261, 314, 318; of displacement (the shifting of one idea to another with no resemblance to the original, except in space or time, and with an often comic effect), 215, 340–44, 444; Plastic representation (visual images of thoughts or concepts, "sometimes also in sensory modalities"), 432; reversals and turning of things and ideas into their opposite, 362; consonance and alliteration, 355.

Language and Thought in Schizophrenia, ed. J. S. Kasanin (New York: Norton, 1964), has an excellent collection of essays, including Norman Cameron, "Experimental Analysis of Schizophrenic Thinking" (on "asyndetic thinking"); Harry Stack Sullivan, "Language of Schizophrenia" (on the schizophrenic's compulsion to talk—for personal security, rather than for communication; on the autistic, narcissistic, individualized nature of unconscious language; on its "magic"); E. Von Domarus, "The Specific Laws of Logic in Schizophrenia" (on paralogic); and Kurt Goldstein, "Methodological Approach to the Study of Schizophrenic Thought Disorder" (on the use of concrete thinking and loss of boundaries between the self and world). On the inability to deal with generalizations in paralogical thought, see E. Hanfmann, "Analysis of the Thinking Disorder in a Case of Schizophrenia," *Archives of Neurology and Psychiatry* 41(1939): 568–79.

See also *American Handbook of Psychiatry*, ed. S. Arieti (New York: Basic Books, 1974); Salomon Resnik, *The Theatre of the Dream*, trans. Alan Sheridan (London: Tavistock Publishers, 1987); Foulkes, *Grammar of Dreams*, Norman Cameron, "The Development of Paranoic Thinking," *Psychology Review* 50 (1943): 219–33; id., "The Paranoic Pseudo-Community," *American Journal of Sociology* 49 (1943): 32–39; J. S. Kasanin, "Me Acute Schizoaffective Psychoses," *American Journal of Psychology* 3 (1937) 97; J. S. Kasanin and E. Hanfmann, "A Method for the Study of Concept Formation," *Journal of Psychology* 3 (1937): 521–40; Gordon Globus, *Dream Life, Wake Life: The Human Condition through Dreams* (Albany: State University of New York, 1987); Antonio R. Damasio, *Descartes' Error: Emotion, Reason and the Human Brain* (New York: Putnam, 1994); and J. Allan Hobson, *The Dreaming Brain* (New York: Basic Books, 1988). For an introduction to these concepts, with illustrations from literature, see Frederick J. Hoffman, *Freudianism and the Literary Mind* (Baton Rouge: Louisiana State University Press, 1945).

3. Colin Duckworth asked Beckett, "Is Lucky so named because he has found his Godot?" Beckett replied, "I suppose he is Lucky to have no more expectations," quoted in Dougald McMillan and Martha Fehsenfeld, *Beckett in the Theatre* (New York: Riverrun Press, 1988), 64.

4. Freud writes of conjunctions, with this his list, 347, in *The Interpretation of Dreams*: "Dreams have no means at their disposal for representing . . . logical relations. . . . The plastic arts of painting and sculpture labour, indeed, under a similar limitation as compared with poetry, which can make use of speech."

5. Beckett listed themes and diagrammed actors' movements in the *Regiebuch*, his production notebook for the 1975 Schiller-Theater production, which he directed. McMillan and Fehsenfeld, in *Beckett in the Theatre* (New York: Riverrun

Press, 1988), have, in a sense, broken the code in deciphering Beckett's often arcane instructions. On the instances of waiting, see 91.

6. E. Von Doramus, "The Specific Laws of Logic in Schizophrenia," in *Language and Thought in Schizophrenia*, 110–11.

7. "I get warm when I run," followed by "quickness, blood, heart of deer, length, driven power, motorized cylinder, strength" is a frequently cited example. In waking, syndetic, or secondary process, all but one or two alternatives in a series would be eliminated; in asyndetic thought, the various alternatives are retained. A statement lacks logical linkage and even the imaginative connective of symbolic statement. See Norman Cameron, "Experimental Analysis of Schizophrenic Thinking," in *Language and Thought in Schizophrenia*, 52–54.

8. Typical of the breakdown of reality boundaries are somatic complaints, which concretely manifest an emotional state—a headache, for example, indicating that one's problems are literally splitting one apart. Estragon's aching feet and Vladimir's pained loins function according to the same mechanism. See *Comprehensive Textbook of Psychiatry*, ed. Alfred M. Freedman et al. (Baltimore: Williams and Wilkins, 1975), I:900.

DECLAN KIBERD

Murphy *and the World of Samuel Beckett*

A medical friend once took Samuel Beckett for a walk in the Dublin hills, hoping to cheer him up. 'It's a beautiful day,' said the friend. 'Oh, it's all right,' grunted the writer. 'No, it's the sort of day that makes you glad to be alive,' insisted the medic, to which Beckett snapped, 'I wouldn't go that far.'[1]

The young artist saw life as a disease, a loss of immortality. Much of the comedy in his world derives from this fish-out-of-water condition, when people are suddenly caught at some disadvantage out of their appropriate role. In Beckett's works, people who regain consciousness do not 'come to'—rather they 'come from'. 'You saved my life,' says a character in his early novel *Murphy* (1938), as if this is a terrible crime: 'now palliate it.'[2] To his dying day, Beckett claimed to be able to recall life in the womb and the trauma of his birth. He felt at times that he had not been fully born, arguing that his inability to get out of bed or out of his mother's house was proof of a womb fixation.

All of this finds an echo not just in the character of Murphy, but also in that of his acquaintance, Cooper, who cannot take off his hat because 'the memories it awoke of the caul were too painful' (69). *Murphy* the novel is set in London, to which Beckett moved in the 1930s after a nervous collapse. He found the transition from Dublin painful. At home, he had been treated as an

From *Samuel Beckett 100 Years: Centenary Essays,* edited by Christopher Murray, pp. 34–47. Published by New Island.

educated gentleman from a good Protestant family; in England he was just another Paddy, so that even simple acts like ordering a meal or buying a paper left him vulnerable to feelings of ridicule. All of this time, Beckett's family tried to goad him into gainful employment, as Celia in the book cajoles her lover Murphy; but he preferred an idle life, mixing with bohemians and prostitutes, saying that he wanted to lie on his back, fart and just think about Dante.

Murphy is a novel of emigration, an attempt to document the plight of those Irish in England who have to contest the image of the Stage Paddy at every turn. Referred to as 'the ruins of the ruins of the broth of a boy' (126), Murphy appears to English onlookers as a bedraggled moron, all body, but his real problem is that he is to himself all mind. He sees himself very justly as a sophisticated, angst-ridden intellectual, but when he goes looking for manual labour, he is mocked as a buffoon. He decides that there is no point in trying to break down the closed system that is the English stereotype of Irishness in 1930s London.

All of Beckett's world is built on closed systems. Murphy's mind is such a system, impenetrable by anyone, even his lover Celia; and so any real form of communication is found to be impossible. The ultimate closed system for Beckett is language itself, used throughout the book to obscure rather than illuminate reality. A character named Quigley is 'a well-to-do ne'er-do-well' (14) and the very circularity of the hyphenated phrases underlines the sense of hopelessness. Great play is made of the similarities between the name Celia and the French phrase '*s'il y a*' (68) but nobody can extract any meaning from the sad pun. It is like a Zen *koan*, something which can only cripple or exhaust the mind which seeks illumination from it.

The novel itself opens with an account of the entire universe as an impermeable code: 'The sun shone, having no alternative, on the nothing new.' A subsequent sentence cuts to Murphy's tragedy of self-deception: 'Murphy sat out of it, as though he were free, in a mew in West Brompton' (5). His error is to believe that he can opt out of this world and attain freedom in his pure mind. Though communication may be impossible, Beckett persists in the belief that other people are still necessary, if only to provide us with a measure of our solitude. There may be self-exile but there is no self-sufficiency.

But Murphy falsely believes that there is and so he sits in his rocking-chair in a daily attempt to find it. The rocking appeases his body, so that he can come alive in the mind. 'And life in his mind gave him pleasure, such pleasure that pleasure was not the word' (6). That cliché will be repeated as an instance of how threadbare phrases can be so worn down as to defeat all communication. Murphy himself is a closed system and great play is made of his non-porous suit, which prevents internal air from escaping or external air from entering, with disastrous results in terms of body odour.

The comedy of non-communication is developed in many ways. Murphy's guru is the Cork mystic Neary, whose surname may be an anagram for 'yearn', but who finds himself just a single link in a chain of futile, star-crossed lovers:

> Of such was Neary's love for Miss Dwyer, who loved a Flight-Lieutenant Elliman, who loved a Miss Farren of Ringaskiddy, who loved a father Fitt of Ballinclashet, who in all sincerity was bound to acknowledge a certain vocation for a Mrs West of Passage, who loved Neary. (7)

The circuit of emotion returns to Neary, but not in a manner which satisfies his or anyone else's desire.

A similar farce of non-reciprocation is developed in much of the novel's dialogue. Typographically, the pages look as if they record conversations, but often upon inspection reveal that it is one person who does all the talking:

> 'Liar,' said Wylie.
>
> This was not a question. Cooper waited for the next question.
>
> 'Neary knows too much,' said Wylie. Cooper waited.
>
> 'You split on him,' said Wylie, 'he splits on you. Isn't that it?' Cooper admitted nothing.
>
> 'All you need,' said Wylie, 'is a little kindness, and in a short time you will be sitting down and taking off your hat and doing all the things that are impossible at present.' (72)

Such passages are effectively soliloquies. They point forward to the monologues of *Molloy* or *Malone Dies*, as well as to the later short plays. The obsession with monologue may be rooted in Beckett's Church of Ireland background, for the Protestant confession is made ultimately to the self, on the basis that every man is his own priest. Because the self can never fully shrive and forgive the self, such monologue is, as Hugh Kenner has said, issueless and potentially endless.[3]

All through *Murphy*, silence is proposed as mankind's destiny. 'Avoid exhaustion by speech' is the counsel given to Murphy on a handbill passed to him by a swami; and the novel might well be read as an almost eastern espousal of quietism. For Murphy, the only way to conquer desire is to ablate it. Silence is his fourth highest attribute; and he ends one chapter listening spellbound to the dead line on a dangling telephone. As the plot unfolds, the many forms of language either stumble or fail completely. Even the terse language of a cryptic telegram becomes confusing: 'LOST STOP STOP WHERE YOU ARE STOP COOPER' (36).

Slips of the tongue are endless. 'O reary Neilly' for 'O really, Neary' or 'Sog. I mean fog'. For his part, Murphy's associate Wylie abandons language as a futile medium when compared with the greater eloquence of bodily gesture, most often a shrug 'that he always used when words were inadequate to conceal what he felt' (75). Beckett well understood the meaning of Oscar Wilde's witticism that everybody is good until they learn how to talk. This ability to obfuscate with words is seen as a particularly Irish gift. When Neary, maddened with unfulfilled desire, tries to dash out his brains on the buttocks of the statue of Cuchulain in the GPO, a Garda says with supreme tautology to the crowd which had gathered to witness the event: 'Move on, [. . .] before yer moved on' (29). The narrator adds: 'It was not in the CG's nature to bandy words, nor had it come into any branch of his training.'

This is true also of Wylie, who shares with many Irish politicians the ability to rob his own sentences of the meaningful climax of a finite verb:

> 'I nearly forgot to say,' he said, 'that when you see Miss Counihan—you will be seeing her, won't you Cooper?'
>
> The skill is really extraordinary with which analphabetes, especially those of Irish education, circumvent their dread of verbal commitments. Now Cooper's face, though it did not seem to move a muscle, brought together and threw off in a single grimace the finest shades of irresolution, revulsion, doglike devotion, catlike discretion, fatigue, hunger, thirst and reserves of strength, in a very small portion of the time that the finest oratory would require for a grossly inferior evasion, and without exposing its proprietor to misquotation. (115)

That long sentence not only suggests that bodily language cannot be misquoted—it also, more significantly, reads like an extended stage direction. It expresses discontent with the limited capacity of words to capture states of feeling and reinforces that sense of discontent with many flashbacks, flashes forward and interpolations. You get the impression of an artist who is straining at the leash in his attempt to break through the conventions of the novel form, in an art which is already halfway to drama, the genre which many years later would ensure Beckett's lasting fame.

On many occasions the narrator breaks down the illusion which has been built up in *Murphy* and he does this with interpolated stage directions. In Chapter Ten, for instance, Neary accidentally kicks a hot-water bottle out of his bed and it bursts, 'so that water is oozing towards the centre of the floor throughout the scene that follows' (117). If *Murphy* is the finest modern attempt to subject the figure of the Stage Irishman to the close psychological analysis made possible by the novel form, then these stagy effects are all the more appropriate as carry-overs from theatre. Many of the exchanges in the book read as if the characters were going through an oft-rehearsed set of speeches:

> 'Everywhere I find defiled,' continued Miss Counihan, 'in the crass and unharmonious unison, the mind at the cart-tail of the body, the body at the chariot-wheels of the mind. I name no names.'
> 'Excellent reception,' said Wylie.
> 'No trace of fading,' said Neary. (122)

This anticipates Pozzo's theatrical description of the sunset in *Waiting for Godot*, as well as his apology at the close: 'I faded a little towards the end.'[4] The narrator of *Murphy* says that all his characters, with the exception of Murphy, are puppets; but that narrator himself seems to be the ultimate puppet, trapped by his pre-existing story into performing a pre-ordained role, as when he apologises for what he must do next—'It is most unfortunate, but the point of this story has been reached where a justification of the expression "Murphy's Mind" has to be attempted' (63). In this way, he shrugs off his duty to propel the plotline forward, even as he seems to submit to his duty to provide a continuing narrative.

The narrator is clearly apologetic and ill at ease in the role, constantly referring to his own problems with the censors or to the difficulties which the typographer will have setting up some capitalised lettering. It is as if the narrator has severe doubts about the validity of the story *and* about his own capacity to find the right words to tell it. What we are offered in the end is not so much a novel written by an author as an imitation of a novel narrated by a man who is nervously impersonating the kind of author he thinks he ought to be. Like all of Beckett's characters, he also feels himself caught between a role and a self. As a novelist he is so unsure that he often lapses into the dramatic form, with stage directions, rehearsed soliloquies and so on. He and his characters are trapped by a script whose words they did not write and by a novel form in which he is fast losing faith: '"If you have news of my love," said Miss Counihan, "speak, speak, I adjure you." She was an omnivorous reader' (69).

Nobody can recall the full script, whose meaning is not wholly understood. In that sense, they all seem like modern puppets who have cut the strings which once bound theirs to God and are therefore left stranded in centre-stage, trying to hold down a role. With the death or loss of God, man seems reduced to inauthentic being and all actions become stagy and hollow, once the divine source of significance is removed. Hence that very modern feeling of a life lived in quotation marks, of being the performer of a role which is understood only by someone else. In Beckett's world, people no longer assert a position, but simply endure a fate.

This novel *Murphy* itself seems to exist in inverted commas, or, as the structuralists would say, perverted commas, being an apologetic recycling of clichés by an author who has no freedom to choose any others but cannot fail to notice their inadequacy. He is a creature of a literary tradition in which he is losing faith. Hence his ferocious parody of a famous passage in James Joyce's *A Portrait of the Artist as a Young Man* where Stephen Dedalus says, 'It was very big to think about everything and everywhere. Only God could do that.'[5] Now, Murphy wonders about the gas fire that will finally take his life: 'Gas. Could it turn a neurotic into a psychotic? No. Only God could do that' (100). Such jibes are based in a sense of despair about the truth-telling powers of literature, as when Neary says cynically to Wylie: 'Let our conversation now be without precedent in fact or literature, each one speaking to the best of his ability the truth to the best of his knowledge' (120). Beckett has in fact so little faith in the power of literature or language that he locates the climax of his novel in a chess-game.

The ultimate indictment of language, however, is the strangely moving but unsatisfactory relationship between Murphy and Celia. 'Celia loved Murphy, Murphy loved Celia, it was a striking case of love requited' (13).

In bed together their heads face opposite ways but they touch beautifully in what the narrator calls 'the short circuit so earnestly desired by Neary' (21). Neary, however, can achieve it only within the closed system of his solitary body, by keeping his toes touching like terminals as he harmonises his yin and yang. This is Beckett's early warning that love between two people may be impossible, since each of us lives and dies alone. That state of self-sufficiency is sought most desperately by those who are still filled with humiliating desires for others. Neary, who 'scratches himself from one itch to the next', envies Murphy his freedom from pangs of unrequited love. When asked what it is that women see in Murphy, Wylie says, 'His surgical quality' (39). As the critic Eugene Webb has noted, those who are slaves to emotion secretly worship Murphy for imperviousness to emotional ties.[6]

Even in his attitude to Celia, Murphy is clinical and physical. Celia is a prostitute. She is presented by the narrator with the suggestion that she, all body, may complement Murphy, all mind. But Murphy only wants her for her heavenly body, summed up in the forename Celia (*caeli*, the heavens); and ultimately he wishes to cure himself of his remaining dependency on Celia, gingerbread and so on, so that he can come alive solely in his mind. '"You, my body, my mind",' he tells her, '"one of these will go, or two, or all. If you, then you only; if my body, then you also; if my mind, then all"' (26–7). Seeking pure mind, he has no use for the world of work, but Celia nags him towards salaried employment, if only to free her from her demeaning profession. So they have endless arguments in which she grows inarticulate with rage, with the result that the hyperliterate Murphy has to complete her sentences for her, her very words of anger against himself. The very words which might signal final parting show instead a couple sharing something as intimate as a single sentence.

Nevertheless, in a book of fast and fluent talkers, Celia's hesitations with language betray a greater honesty. Her silences suggest that she may be the most sensitive person of them all, unimpressed by Murphy's glib facility with language:

> She felt, as she felt so often with Murphy, spattered with words that went dead as soon as they sounded; each word obliterated, before it had time to make sense, by the word that came next; so that in the end she did not know what had been said. It was like difficult music heard for the first time. (27)

Celia finds such words to be pure sound devoid of meaning, a version of the MUSIC, MUSIC MUSIC in ascending capitals (132) which they share every night. That capitalised phrase is as near as the Irish censors will permit the narrator go to an account of sexual intercourse, another breakdown of language. But the clearest and most poignant example of that breakdown is Murphy's failure to explain to Celia why he must not go to work. The more he explains, the less she understands. Only when she shares his tranquil silence in the rocking-chair does light begin to dawn on her: 'she began to understand as soon as he gave up trying to explain' (42).

The trouble with this is that it means she must go back to her prostitute's beat, in order to support Murphy in his reveries; and if she must sell her body to other men, then there can be no more music with Murphy. At this argument, Murphy's patience breaks and he asks whether what they feel is love: '"What do you love? [. . .] Me as I am? You can want what does not exist, you can't love it. Then why are you all out to change me? So you won't have to love me?"' (25). He fears, like many men, that his partner wants to change the very thing in him with which she originally fell in love. He fears that what she really loves are her own reasons for loving him, an ideal image of herself as prostitute-turned-respectable-housewife and social reformer. Murphy suspects that her love for him is really an aspect of her love for herself and that what she really esteems is the opportunity he may provide. This is the tragic theme at the heart of every Beckett text—people exist only in their need for one another and use one another as pawns in games of self-love. If Celia worships Murphy for his surgical quality, it is simply in hopes that from him she can learn the art of self-sufficiency, as indeed she does at the end, once she enters the trance made possible by the rocking-chair.

Even when two people share aspirations, Beckett suggests that they can never manage to synchronise them. Celia understands Murphy's need for indolence, but only after her nagging has driven him away. In the last pages, he makes a fleeting resolve to return to Celia, but by then she has achieved self-sufficiency in the chair. In such a world of isolated persons, the idea of desire for another is not only impractical—it is also utterly laughable. And the only way to find peace is to adopt the eastern philosophy of emptying oneself of the desire for created things.

In this context, Murphy must stand convicted of rank hypocrisy, for in the final chapter he violates this moral code on a number of occasions. His last will and testament—indicating that his ashes should be flushed down a toilet at the Abbey Theatre, itself founded to put an end to the Stage Irishman—is in turn a sin, since it involves the act of wishing or desiring something. In fact, it is flagrantly in defiance of his own code, since the will is based on a wish to implement one's desires even after death. It is fitting that this sin should be punished by non-fulfilment, for Murphy's ashes are not in fact scattered down the loo of the Abbey Theatre but rather across the floor of a sawdust pub in London, a place in which the Stage Irishman was often presented as part of a popular entertainment.

Even more serious, however, is the way in which Murphy breaches his own code in his dealings with Mr Endon, an amiable schizophrenic who has already achieved that very self-enclosure of which Murphy still dreams. For Murphy, who has taken work as an orderly at a mental hospital, the psychiatric patients are all heroes who have won the battle for self-sufficiency. What the psychiatrists call exile, he calls sanctuary, and he sees the patients 'not as banished from a system of benefits but as escaped from a colossal fiasco' (101). He tries to learn the secret of self-sufficiency from Mr Endon in a chess-game they play. However, Mr Endon offers no response to Murphy's moves, failing to capture any of Murphy's men, even when Murphy tries his best to lose some. In truth, Mr Endon is entirely unaware of his chess partner. In the end, as Murphy looks into Mr Endon's eye, he sees reflected back just his own image, distorted and reduced on Mr Endon's eyeball.

In other words, Murphy looks hopefully at Mr Endon for some sign of recognition, only to see himself and his own predicament mirrored in Mr Endon's inability to see anything except himself. Just as Celia received only a reduced and distorted image of herself back from Murphy, so now he suffers the same fate at the hands of Mr Endon. To be is, indeed, to be perceived by some other. Moreover, in his approach to Mr Endon, Murphy is guilty of the same hypocrisy of which he had once accused Celia. He had complained that she was guilty of trying to change the very thing in him which she claimed to love, but this is precisely what he is doing to Mr Endon. What he most admires and wishes to emulate is Mr Endon's self-sufficiency; yet it is this self-sufficiency which he seeks to break down in his search for a flicker of recognition from the patient. If Mr Endon had responded, it would have been a catastrophe, for Murphy would have effectively destroyed the one remaining human quality which he claimed to prize above all others.

Murphy's death may be seen in these terms as a fitting punishment for his misdemeanour, and for his failure to appreciate the true situation of the mental patients. Whereas Mr Endon to Murphy was bliss, to Mr Endon he was no more than chess, his eye no more than the 'chessy eye' (135). The opening pages of the book had warned us that Murphy's desire to escape the world of time and contingency was a gross self-deceit. At the start, Murphy sat out of the sun, apart from the measurer of time, 'as though he were free' (5). But he is not at all free of the world: on the second page of the novel that illusion of freedom was described as a fond hope. So, at the end he is shown to have utterly misinterpreted the very real sufferings of the Magdalen Mental Mercyseat patients, not realising that he was 'walking round and round at the foot of the cross' (132) each time he performed his hospital rounds and peered through the Judas hole at the lunatics in their cells. He falsely believed that the patients were having 'a glorious time', but the narrator insists that the narrator had to fight hard to maintain this interpretation against the pressure of actual experience at the hospital: 'Nothing remained but to substantiate these [impressions], distorting all that threatened to belie them. It was strenuous work, but very pleasant' (100).

The deception is finally unmasked. Murphy's trendy modern urge to sentimentalise the deranged as the possessor of higher wisdom is shown to be false. He returns to his own death in the knowledge that, as Virginia Woolf wrote, 'we perish, each alone.' Whether Murphy's death is by suicide or by accident is perhaps of no great account. Some critics point to the fact that Murphy must have resolved to die since he speaks his last words consciously and deliberately as a final utterance:

> the last at last seen of him
> himself unseen by him
> and of himself (140)

Others suggest that, since he decides on a return visit to the flat he shared with Celia at Brewery Road, he has in fact abandoned his illusions about Mr Endon and is ready to return to her. Hence, they claim, the death is a bizarre accident brought on by his absent-mindedness in releasing the gas. It scarcely matters, for by now Celia has lost all interest in the outside world, having perfected the art of coming alive in the mind in her rocking-chair. There is no real need for the narrator to describe her final state of mind, because this has already been done in the account given of Murphy's experience in the rocking-chair in Chapter Six. *This* is, in fact, his real last will—the knowledge of the futility of the workaday world bequeathed at last to the Celia who will take his place.

Like Joyce's *A Portrait of the Artist as a Young Man* this book also offers a tale of a sensitive hero who is left with nobody to talk to but himself. Both books also suggest that the more sensitive a person is, the less likely he is to be able to share that sensitivity with others. Language is a poor, blunt instrument at best and its imperfections would make all honest men and women wince. At the inquest on Murphy, there is a final abuse of language, when a Dr Killiecrankie pronounces Murphy's passing 'A classical case of misadventure' (147). This leads the narrator to make the acid comment: 'words never failed Dr Killiecrankie, that for him would have been tantamount to loose thinking' (147). By a delicious irony, which goes to underwrite Beckett's philosophy that life is a loss of immortality, it turns out that Murphy's remains can be identified only by a birthmark, which thus turns out also to be a death mark.

There are times when the novel almost grinds to a complete halt because of the hyper-sensitive narrator's finicky precision with words and because of his distrust of any word that seems not quite right, which is to say most words. But he persists to the end in telling Murphy's story and that is Beckett's final resting-point. Beckett fully understands the temptation which assails all vulnerable people, to end the unsatisfactory charade of communication with others and lapse into a private world of exquisite sensitivity to the self. That is Murphy's terrible mistake, to think that in the modern world it is enough to defend a private sensibility. But Beckett to his dying day persisted, despite all the odds, in the attempt to communicate something, if only man's sense of loneliness. In fact, he made failure and destitution his major themes. In that, he was a truly Irish author with links right back to those Gaelic bards who, after the collapse of their order in 1600, wrote poems of utter dejection announcing the death of Irish. But they proclaimed this death in lines of such throbbing power as to rebut their very message. They couldn't go on, they said, but went on anyway. Likewise with Beckett. In his writings, all language seems to die, but it records its own demise with such honesty and exactitude as to leave some grounds for hope. Not for nothing did Beckett like to quote a line from Shakespeare's darkest play, *King Lear.* 'The worst is not, / So long as we can say "This is the worst"' (IV.i.25–26). For to be able to describe the collapse of language and culture suggests a mind still able to formulate the sense of cultural crisis: and to be able to formulate suggests, however dimly, the hope of recovery. For these reasons, it would be wrong to call Beckett a nihilist. Long before R.D. Laing and the anti-psychiatrists of the 1960s sought to sentimentalise the mentally ill, Beckett understood that such illness is never enviable and often deeply tragic. He had fought his own way back from depression and learned how to report it with clarity; the findings of that report are chronicled with matchless authority in what may well be his most underrated book, *Murphy.* It is also one of his funniest books, for as its author was to write twenty years later: 'nothing is funnier than unhappiness'.[7]

Notes

1. For a different version of this story, which carries the force of folklore, see John Calder, *The Philosophy of Samuel Beckett* (London: Calder Publications, 2001), p. 12.
2. Samuel Beckett, *Murphy* (London: Pan Books, in association with Calder & Boyars, 1973), p. 36. Subsequent quotations from *Murphy* are from this edition, to which page numbers in parentheses refer.
3. Hugh Kenner, *A Reader's Guide to Samuel Beckett* (London: Thames and Hudson, 1973), p. 134.
4. Samuel Beckett, *The Complete Dramatic Works* (London: Faber & Faber, 1990), p. 38.
5. James Joyce, *A Portrait of the Artist as a Young Man* (Harmondsworth: Penguin, 1960), p. 16.
6. Eugene Webb, *Samuel Beckett: A Study of His Novels* (London: Peter Owen, 1970) p. 49.
7. *Endgame*, in *The Complete Dramatic Works*, p. 101.

ERIC P. LEVY

Disintegrative Process in Endgame

Endgame is a play about process: "Something is taking its course" (13, 32). On one level, that elapsing process concerns the performance of the play itself; as many critics have noted, *Endgame* foregrounds its own status as a drama through a variety of devices: (a) Hamm's name (which, according to Hugh Kenner, denotes "an actor"; 1968, 00); (b) Hamm's reference to playing ("Me—to play" [END, 2]); (c) Clov's elaborate uncurtaining of the props and windows prior to speaking; and (d) the references to theatrical terms such as *dialogue* (58), *aside* (77), *soliloquy* (78), *underplot* (78), *exit* (81), and performative *technique* (59; Kenner 1968, 156). Hannah Copeland sums up this reflexive emphasis: "Here the focus upon the play as play is relentless" (1975, 48).[1]

But with his opening soliloquy, Clov indicates another kind of process, one whose commencement precedes his appearance on stage and does not rely on dramatic convention: "Finished, it's finished, nearly finished, it must be nearly finished. (*Pause.*) Grain upon grain, one by one, suddenly, there's a heap, a little heap, the impossible heap" (END, 1). Later, Hamm echoes these observations and deepens their significance: "It's finished, we're finished. Nearly finished" (50); "Moment upon moment, pattering down, like the millet grains of . . . that old Greek, and *all life long you wait for that to mount up to a life*" (70; my emphasis). As Hamm's remarks suggest, this alternate process

From *Trapped in Thought: A Study of the Beckettian Mentality*, pp. 162–79.

concerns the lived experience of time or, in alternate formulation, the temporality of living. Yet here the process of living entails not the continuous unfolding of the intrinsic meaning or value of the animate subject in question, but only the accumulation of temporal units that remain extraneous to the subject enduring through them.

The Problematic Relation of Whole to Parts

The deeper implications of this view of life emerge when we investigate Hamm's allusion to "that old Greek." As several critics have noted, the philosopher cited is Zeno of Elea, who flourished around 450 B.C.[2] The imagery regarding falling grain occurs in one of Zeno's many arguments (technically, *reductiones ad absurdum*) against Pythagorean pluralism and in support of Parmenidean monism: If the *parts* (i.e., the grains) of a bushel of corn make no sound when falling, how can the *whole* (i.e., the entire bushel) make a sound when falling, since it is composed entirely of its parts? Through reasoning that Aristotle (who reports it) has no trouble refuting, Zeno here attempts (a) to demonstrate the logical absurdity of postulating parts, and hence, (b) to prove that reality is a plenum or indivisible and unitary whole (*Physics* 7.5.250a20–24).

An inversion of the same problem constitutes the thematic core of *Endgame*. Whereas Zeno problematized plurality and multiplicity, *Endgame* begins by problematizing indivisible wholeness. In this Beckettian context, life itself is the problematic whole. How can a whole life be made of such parts as both Clov and Hamm cite: "[A]ll life long you wait for that to mount up to a life"? Under these conditions, where the whole is negated by the meaningless accumulation of its temporal parts, life can no longer be construed as a continuous process of becoming by which the living individual progressively unfolds his or her significance: "Mean something! You and I, mean something! Ah that's a good one!" (END, 33). But if life comprises meaningless parts, or what Hamm terms "moments for nothing" (83), then the *time* in which life endures or elapses can no longer be defined as a cumulative succession of consecutive instants. In this sense, "time is over": "Moments for nothing, now as always, time was never and time is over, reckoning closed and story ended" (83). Instead of cumulative succession effecting continuous transition from past to future, time here paradoxically perpetuates its own irrelevance: "The end is in the beginning and yet you go on" (69).

In this context, as Clov indicates when answering Hamm's question, "What time is it?" time is always "[t]he same as usual" (END, 4). But if time merely perpetuates its own constancy and always remains the same as usual, then the passage of time can accomplish no more than the accumulation of identical units. Thus, instead of the eventual combination of parts into a whole (as in Hamm's waiting for granular moments "to mount up to a life"), the passage of time entails the continuous disintegration of the whole into its parts, which are then abandoned or withdrawn, as in one of Clov's "visions" (41): "I am so bowed I only see my feet, if I open my eyes, and *between my legs a little trail of black dust*" (81; my emphasis). This condition recalls Molloy's dictum: "To decompose is to live too" (MOL, 25).

Disintegrative process in *Endgame* is epitomized by sequential loss of parts. There are no more "bicycle wheels" (END, 8), "sugarplums" (55), "navigators" (65), "rugs" (67), or "coffins" (77). There is no more "pap" (9), "nature" (11), "tide" (62), or "painkiller" (71). Eventually, as Hamm indicates, "there'll be no more wall any more. Infinite emptiness will be all around you, all the resurrected dead of all the ages wouldn't fill it, and there you'll be like a little bit of grit in the middle of the steppe" (36). In this remarkable image of time as the agent of divestiture, the whole is evacuated of all content but a single residual part, "a little bit of grit in the middle of the steppe": subjectivity stranded in "infinite emptiness" (36). But the emptiness here indicated pertains not to the external world but to the internal one. The temporal process of divestiture or evacuation deprives subjectivity of its own content until all that remains is awareness of lack or deprivation. This is the quintessential suffering represented by Beckettian mimesis: "[Y]our heart bleeds you lose your heart drop by drop weep even an odd tear inward no sound" (HOW, 23, 66). It is graphically formulated Hamm: "There's something dripping in my head. A heart, a heart in my head" (END, 18).

The Mimesis of a Mentality

At this point, it is crucial to recognize that the setting of *Endgame* corresponds precisely to the paradigm of subjectivity stranded in "infinite emptiness." That is, the setting localizes a *mentality*, not a place, and the mentality in question is defined by preoccupation with loss and depletion. Of course, to situate the setting in a mental context is not a new suggestion, though it contradicts the opinion of such critics as Vivian Mercier, Theodore Adorno, and S. E. Gontarski, who have respectively identified the barren outer world in *Endgame* with postnuclear devastation; post-Holocaust depredation; and the war-ravaged Picardy-Normandy landscape, which Beckett himself—a volunteer ambulance driver for the Irish Red Cross—regularly drove through in 1945 (Mercier 1977, 174; Adorno 1969, 9–40; Gontarski 1985, 33). Regarding the relation between setting and mind, Hugh Kenner long ago noted that "the stage, with its high peepholes [seems] to be the inside of an immense skull" (1968, 155). Per Nykrog cites a nineteenth-century literary practice of construing "room" as a symbol for the mind (1998, 124). Moreover, Beckett's art makes frequent reference to mental as opposed to physical setting: "We are needless to say in a skull" (CAL, 38). The *Texts* narrator locates himself "inside an imaginary head" (TFN, 82) and then explicitly distinguishes that mental being from bodily existence: "What can have become then of the tissues I was, I can see them no more, feel them no more, flaunting and fluttering all about and inside me, pah they must be still on their old prowl somewhere, passing themselves off as me" (TFN, 103). The narrator of "From an Abandoned Work" applies a similar formula: "just went on, my body doing its best without me" (FAAW, 49).

Once it is recognized that the setting of *Endgame* is mental, the obliteration of the external world ("[z]ero" [END, 29]) and the extermination of everything living in it ("corpsed" [30]) gain new meaning. For in this context, the emphasis on external vacancy signifies not the literal destruction of the outer world but the inability or refusal of the mentality represented to acknowledge anything outside the concerns preoccupying its own interiority: "To hell with the universe" (46). Since these concerns fundamentally involve awareness of lack or depletion, the emptiness of the external world in the play is no more than the objective correlative of internal awareness. That is, the outer world becomes the reification of awareness of inner emptiness—an objectification of a habitual perspective or way of seeing. Indeed, the play foregrounds the role of perspective in defining the outer world, as in the example of the madman who, when invited to look through the window at "[a]ll that loveliness," recoiled "[a]ppalled" for "[a]ll he had seen was ashes" (44). The role of perspective in determining the meaning of what is seen appears also in Clov's observing through the wrong window: "Ah what a fool I am! I'm on the wrong side!" (73). In noting his error, he associates it with mental aberration: "Sometimes I wonder if I'm in my right senses. Then it passes off and I'm as intelligent as ever" (73).

To observe that *Endgame* is (to adapt the Unnamable's phrasing) set in "a head abandoned to its ancient solitary resources" (UN, 361) is to approach the play as the mimesis of a mentality or psychological orientation toward life. Viewed from this angle, the characters in the play constitute contrapuntal expressions of the same persistent mentality. Indeed, according to James Knowlson, when Beckett directed a German production of *Endgame* (Endspiel) in 1967, he described the play as "full of echoes; they all answer each other" (1996, 551). The hallmark of this mentality is obsessive concern with interior distress to the exclusion of all other considerations. For example, there is never anything in Hamm's world but the sense of its irrelevance: "It all happened without me" (END, 74).[3] The only object of his continuous attention is himself. "Well, there we are, there I am, that's enough" (83). No other object can compete with or displace preoccupation with his own suffering that abides "in the center" (25) of his awareness: "Can there be misery—loftier than mine?" (2). What never changes for Hamm is obsession with the malaise of his own interiority: "Last night I saw inside my breast. There was a big sore" (32).

The Primacy of Habit

Experience in *Endgame* is dominated by the same principle of inescapable interiority as that formulated by Beckett in *Proust*: "We are alone. We cannot know and we cannot be known. 'Man is the creature that cannot come forth from himself, who knows others only in himself, and who, if he asserts the contrary, lies'" (P, 66). Yet, whereas according to the doctrine formulated in *Proust* isolation is imposed as an ontological condition of human being, in *Endgame* it arises from mental habit perpetuated over time. The play indicates that, at any age, Hamm resorts to the same mental habits—to the point that, as a character, he does not so much represent a person as incarnate a mental habit that can inhabit or, at least, influence any susceptible host. This dispensation reinforces our earlier observation that the play concerns the mimesis of an attitude or mentality.

However, the suggestion that the play dramatizes a persistent mental habit, regarding which (to interpolate Vladimir's phrase in *Waiting for Godot*) "The essential doesn't change" (WFG, 14), contradicts Jennifer Jeffers's claim (derived from the philosophical writings of Deleuze and Guatarri) that Beckett's art depicts "[t]he plane of immanence [which] does not represent an idea [but] . . . instead . . . presents the event, the discourse, the becoming or the flow" (Jeffers 1996, 65).[4] According to this view, Beckettian mimesis represents "thought . . . cut loose from representation," "an immanent plane where thinking is not restricted" by traditional categories of conceptualization, "where language stops and the pure image of thought begins" (Jeffers 1996, 66, 67). But far from concerning the pure flow of thought, abstracted from the structure of its own content, the mentality represented in *Endgame* remains imprisoned in its structure. Here thought can only reiterate through time the pattern of its own habitual operation.

The emphasis on habit in *Endgame* is relentless: "But I feel too old, and too far, to form new habits" (END, 81). Indeed, in response to Clov's question regarding repetitious practice ("Why this farce, day after day?"), Hamm identifies the cause as "[r]outine" (32). In *Proust*, Beckett defined habit as "An automatic adjustment of the human organism to the conditions of its existence" (P, 20). According to this theory, much invoked by critics, the life of an individual sustains routine patterns that insulate against the destabilizing intrusion of change, until factors beyond the control of the individual alter the circumstances of personal existence, requiring the construction of a new habit after an excruciating "period of transition" (P, 21).[5]

The relationship between Hamm and Clov corresponds to that between an individual and the habit by which "automatic adjustment of the human organism to the conditions of its existence" is achieved. In *Proust*, Beckett refers to habit as a "minister of dullness" and "agent of security" (P, 21) that is "tophatted and hygienic" (28). Clov is obsessed with domestic order ("I love order" [END, 57]) and, near the end of the play, sports a "Panama hat" (82). But the link between Clov and habit is reinforced in another way. In *Proust*, habit is compared to a "cook . . . who knows what has to be done, and will slave all day and all night rather than tolerate any redundant activity in the kitchen" (P, 20). When not with Hamm, Clov retires to his kitchen: "I'll go now to my kitchen" (END, 2). Since Clov is thus associated with the ministrations of habit, it follows that the departure of Clov, near the end of the play, signifies "the death of Habit and the brief suspension of its vigilance" (P, 23), initiating one of "the perilous zones in the life of the individual" suddenly bereft of habit (P, 19). Indeed, just before exiting, Clov refers to both reliance on habit ("But I feel too old, and too far, to form new habits" [END, 81]), and the sudden entry into the transitional period, "when for a moment the boredom of living [under the care of habit] is replaced by the suffering of being" (P, 19): "Then one day, suddenly, it ends, it changes" (END, 81). Hence, Hamm alone is Hamm without his "current habit of living" (P, 20). Hamm alone is Hamm suffering one of "these periods of abandonment" by habit, when the task is "to create a new habit that will empty the mystery of its threat" (P, 22).

But Hamm alone displays none of the suffering of being that Beckett in *Proust* associates with the period of transition. On the contrary, as soon as he realizes that Clov is gone, Hamm repeats the words with which, at the outset of the play, he initiated his "[r]outine" (32) with Clov: "Me—to play" (END, 2, 82). But this time, instead of issuing imperatives to Clov, he applies them to himself "Discard" (82), "Take it easy" (82), "Raise hat" (82), "And put on again" (82), "Discard" (84), "speak no more" (84). Hamm concludes by covering his face with the handkerchief so that he resumes the "attitude" (55) with which, at the commencement of the play, he began. Hamm is immune to change because, as Clov observes, he perpetuates the same state, whatever his external circumstances: "All life long the same questions, the same answers" (5); "All life long the same inanities" (45). Hamm has always been like this, despite modification of local conditions. For no matter where he is, Hamm is never there: "Absent, *always*. It all happened without me" (74; my emphasis). His blindness epitomizes his obliviousness to change. As Pozzo declares in *Waiting for Godot*, "The blind have no notion of time. The things of time are hidden from them too" (WFG, 55). Indeed, the similarity between the series of imperatives uttered here by Hamm and the sequential stage directions reinforces the notion of immunity to change. For just as, on the theatrical level, the purpose of a play is to be performed again and again, so the purpose of habit is to ensure repetition of the thoughts and actions that constitute it.

Habit and Automatism

In *Endgame*, character is reduced to habit, defined in *Proust* as "[a]n automatic adjustment of the human organism to the conditions of its existence" (P, 20). That is, according to Beckett, "Life is habit" (P, 19), and habit is determined by what Leo Spitzer, in a different context, refers to as "automatism": a mechanism with its own automatic—or, as we might say today, programmed—configuration of operation (1948, 149). In the play, that which is "taking its course" (END, 13, 32) is what the narrator of *How It Is* terms "the force of habit" (HOW, 47), construed here as automatic process, proceeding with the same mechanical inevitability as the ticking of the "alarm-clock" that Clov "hangs up" on the wall (END, 72). For, according to "the law of automatism," as formulated by Spitzer, "once the first step is taken the process must run its course" (1948, 149). To interpolate Hamm's phrasing, "The end is in the beginning" (END, 69), and once the process begins, it must continue to completion.

Ironically, the moment in the play where automatic process is most emphasized, reducing character to purely rote activity without emotional involvement, occurs when Clov responds "tonelessly" and with "fixed gaze" to Hamm's request to say "Something . . . from your heart" (END, 80). Here, just as, according to the *Proust* essay, "life is habit" (P, 19), so too love is habit—the operation of an impersonal automatism. More precisely, because life is habit whose pattern of response is "pre-established" (MOL, 62), there can be no love: "never loved anything" (HOW, 41). Similarly, in *Endgame* the love of God, as manifested through prayer, is also reduced to the operation of habit, understood as a pattern of response that continues automatically once initiated: "Off we go" (END, 55). Indeed, Nagg's mode of prayer parodies mechanical response, "Nagg (clasping his hands, closing his eyes, in a gabble): Our Father which art—" (55). An analogous instance of mechanical prayer (and one that, as Knowlson has noted, corresponds to an extant photograph of the very young Beckett with his mother on the veranda of Cooldrinagh, the family home) occurs in *How It Is*: "in a word bolt upright on a cushion whelmed in a nightshirt I pray according to her instructions" (Knowlson 1996, 462; HOW, 15).

With respect to automatism in *Endgame*, there are only two alternatives: "[w]inding up" (END, 72) and running down: "One day you'll say, I'm tired, I'll stop" (37); "Then one day, suddenly, it ends, it changes, I don't understand, it dies, or it's me, I don't understand, that either" (81). Love is irrelevant in this environment, for love here is not a feeling but just another activity performed according to memorized procedure: "Get out of here and love one another! Lick your neighbour as yourself!" (68). Moreover, love requires communication, and words themselves are the product of regularized intercourse, not spontaneous intimacy: "I use the words you taught me. If they don't mean anything any more, teach me others. Or let me be silent" (44); "I ask the words that remain—sleeping, waking, morning, evening. They have nothing to say" (83).[6] Nor can there be compassion in this environment, for when life is governed by a pattern of regularity, the suffering of others must either be assimilated to supervenient routine (as in the hospice for those "dying of their wounds" [80]) or ignored as efficaciously as possible: "Bottle him!" (10). Moreover, in a world ruled by automatism, emotion—the *sine qua non* of compassion—is subordinated to and eventually displaced by regularized performance: "Every man his specialty" (10).

Perhaps the supreme symbol in Beckettian art for the reduction of life to automatism is the timepiece, whether watch, clock, or timer-bell. A short list of examples will foreground the issue: (a) Clov (as already noted) hanging an "alarm-clock" on the wall (END, 70) and then placing it "on lid of Nagg's bin" (79); (b) Pozzo referring to his watch ("A genuine half-hunter"), whose ticking, in the scene where Vladimir and Estragon attempt to locate it, is eventually confused with his own heartbeat: "It's the heart" (WFG, 30); (c) Winnie required to conduct her stationary existence "between the bell for waking and the bell for sleep" (HD, 21); (d) the narrator in *How It Is* referring to "Pim's timepiece" and the "ticking" of "a big ordinary watch with heavy chain" (HOW, 40, 58); (e) Molloy referring to his own life as a "[w]atch wound and buried by the watchmaker"—that is, as a "mechanism" that functions according to a "pre-established" pattern of operation, thus rendering personal responsibility for fulfillment in life irrelevant (MOL, 36, 51, 62).

In the context of automatism, Clov's placing of the alarm clock on the lid of Nagg's ashbin is especially significant. For time is indeed superfluous ("time is over" [END, 83]) in an environment where time is always "the same as usual" (4) because its moments are the measure of mechanical process, configured to follow a series of predetermined movements until concluding, as epitomized in "For To End Yet Again": "for to end yet again by degrees or *as though switched on*" (FTEYA, 15; my emphasis). Moreover, the primacy of automatism also clarifies the emphasis in *Endgame* on "the play as play" (to recall Copeland's phrase, quoted at the outset). For construed in strictly performative terms, a play is an automatism, designed to run to the end once it begins—and then to begin again on another occasion: "Through it who knows yet another end" (FTEYA, 15). Just as, to quote Hamm once again, "[t]he end is in the beginning" (END, 69), so the beginning of the next performance of the play is foreshadowed in the end. Hamm replaces the same handkerchief on his face at the end of the play as that which Clov removed from his face at the beginning.

Thus, in *Endgame*, automatism does not merely take its course. For once it has run down, it must begin again. Through this notion of redundant automatism, Beckett modifies the concept of habit enunciated in *Proust*: "[L]ife is a succession of habits, since the individual is a succession of individuals [each defined through the habits proper to him]" (P, 19). Whereas in *Proust* Beckett gave equal emphasis to habits and the "periods of transition" (P, 19) between them, in *Endgame*, by implication, he eliminates the transitional intervals between consecutive habits. Transition now has no significance other than the beginning of a new automatism—or the renewing of an old one: "To think that in a moment all will be said, all to do again" (CAL, 44).

The purpose of automatism in Beckettian mimesis is to reduce thinking to mechanical process ("But there is reasoning somewhere. . . . It's mechanical" [TFN, 117]) so that the mind can be excused from attending to its own content: "[W]hat's the matter with my head, I must have left it in Ireland, in a saloon" (TFN, 113). The celebrated upshot of this strategy is the predicament where the narrator's awareness is distracted by the audition of a voice whose identity he cannot determine but which, in fact, articulates his own thinking: "He knows they are words, he is not sure they are his" (UN, 354). This condition epitomizes the Beckettian "sense of absence" (MAL, 279)—a condition Hamm applies to himself ("Absent, always. It all happened without me" [END, 74]). When first citing this passage, we interpreted it in terms of Hamm's mental withdrawal from *external* circumstances. We can now see that, at a deeper level, it signifies Hamm's withdrawal from his *mental* circumstances. That is, Beckettian mimesis gives new meaning to the term *absent-mindedness*. For here absent-mindedness ("my mind absent, elsewhere" [TFN, 108]) ultimately pertains to the absence of the mind from its own thought in order thereby to achieve "flight from self" (UN, 367): "I say to the head, Leave it alone, stay quiet, it stops breathing, then pants on worse than ever. I am far from all that wrangle, I shouldn't bother with it" (TFN, 75).

The Provenance of Automatist Process

The play appears to derive this strategy from childhood. Nagg recalls Hamm's nocturnal fear of abandonment: "Whom did you call when you were a tiny boy, and were frightened, in the dark? Your mother? No. Me. We let you cry. Then we moved you out of earshot, so that we might sleep in peace" (END, 56). Hamm refers to the habitual tactic of "the solitary child" to insulate itself from the threat of isolation: "Then babble, babble, words, like the solitary child who turns himself into children, two, three, so as to be together, and whisper together, in the dark" (70). After discovering that he has been abandoned by Clov, Hamm again invokes the plight of the solitary child: "You cried for night; it falls: now cry in darkness" (83).[7] The strategy of absent-mindedness through automatism can be construed as an elaboration of childhood recourse to conversation with imaginary friends. In this context, the "babble, babble" by which "the solitary child" populates his loneliness ultimately becomes the automatist flow of thought by which the mind withdraws attention, not only from the world of which it is aware, but also from its own awareness in order thereby to achieve complete insularity—a state symbolized by Hamm's retirement behind the bloody "Veronica," which he drapes over his face: "Old stauncher! You remain" (84).

The only factor that can overcome the need for subjective isolation is "compassion" (END, 76). But here we encounter a Beckettian double bind. Lack of compassion forces the subject to seek escape from his predicament. Yet compassion would condemn others to endure even longer their own plight. This unusual circumstance is dramatically expressed in Hamm's reproach of the peasant father who beseeched Hamm to "consent to take in" both the peasant father and his "child" (53): "He doesn't realize, all he knows is hunger, and cold, and death to crown it all. But you! You ought to know what the earth is like, nowadays. Oh I put him before his responsibilities!" (83).

Here Hamm indicates that the father's request for a shelter put his own need for survival before concern for the suffering that survival would force his son to endure. Yet, despite this opinion, Hamm apparently did admit Clov as a child into his abode. When he asks whether Clov can "remember when you came," the reply is "No. Too small you told me" (END, 38). As Hamm's ward, Clov has learned his lesson well; he actually refines Hamm's rejection of compassion. Brief analysis of Clov's celebrated remark will clarify: "If I don't kill that rat he'll die" (68). As an inversion of the tautology "If I kill that rat he'll die," the statement epitomizes the Beckettian ethic in *Endgame*. Compassion is meaningless. The preservation of life only prolongs a condition of terminal futility. Hence, pity and cruelty coincide.

There are only two types of people in *Endgame*: parents or parental substitutes, and their children or wards. Nagg and Nell are respectively Hamm's father and mother. Hamm "was a father to" Clov (END, 38); Hamm's elaborate story concerns a father and son. The figure of the abandoned or neglected child is especially emphasized: (a) Hamm as "a tiny boy" banished "out of earshot" at night so that his parents "might sleep in peace" (56); (b) the peasant's child temporarily left "all alone" while his father journeys to beg Hamm for succor (52); and (c) the "small boy" suddenly spotted by Clov and ignored by Hamm: "If he exists he'll die there or he'll come here" (78). Thus established as a dominant motif, the abandoned or neglected child is the ultimate source or *locus classicus* of the sense of absence and "infinite emptiness" (36).

In this context, Hamm's recourse to discarding possessions at the end of the play makes more sense. The abandoned child has himself been discarded and so can find protection only through identifying with discarding. All that he retains is the sense of deprivation and the need to withdraw from the uncaring world ("Outside of here it's death" [9]) into his own interiority—and ultimately, as we have seen, even *from* that interiority.

In Beckettian art, the supreme expression of parental indifference concerns the nativity scene in *Company*: "A mother stooping over cradle from behind. She moves aside to let the father look. In his turn he murmurs to the newborn. Flat tone unchanged. *No trace of love*" (COM, 66; my emphasis). Here the utter absence of parental love alters the project of the child, whose task is to satisfy "the craving for company"—not through seeking the love forever withheld, but by "devising figments to temper his nothingness" (COM, 77, 64). The same project motivates the narrator of *Texts for Nothing*, in a passage that constitutes an apt gloss on Hamm's predicament at the conclusion of *Endgame*: "I'm in my arms, I'm holding myself in my arms, without much tenderness, but faithfully, faithfully. Sleep now, as under that ancient lamp, all twined together, tired out with so much talking, so much listening, so much toil and play" (TFN, 79).

Paradoxically, in the Beckettian universe the greatest need of the mentality formed by the sense of abandonment and neglect suffered by "the solitary child" is to sustain the state of isolation. In that circumstance no further rejection can ever intrude, since the only companions are the figures whom "the solitary child turns himself into" through fantasy (END, 70). In alternate formulation, the isolation experienced in childhood simply becomes a habit that experience cannot break. On the model of the parent–child relationship, intimacy is construed as reciprocal estrangement, as in the *Texts* narrator's account of walks with his father as a boy: "[W]e walked together, hand in hand, silent, sunk in our worlds, each in his worlds, the hands forgotten in each other" (TFN, 79). Analogous accounts occur in *The Unnamable* ("each one in his little elsewhere" [UN, 403]) and *Ohio Impromptu* ("so long alone together" [OI, 14]).

The Problematics of Love

The fundamental source of the "misery" (END, 2) in the play concerns love or, more precisely, its lack. The overwhelming power of love to affect the mind is formally enunciated in *Words and Music*: "Love is of all the passions the most powerful passion and indeed no passion is more powerful than the passion of love. That is the mode in which the mind is most strongly affected and indeed in no mode is the mind more strongly affected than this" (WM, 24). In the Beckettian environment, as indicated by the narrator of *How It Is*, love cannot be distinguished from the fear of abandonment: "love fear of being abandoned a little of each no knowing" (HOW, 66). That is, because of "the well-known mechanism of association" (MOL, 48), whose operation is founded on bitter experience (obliquely suggested in the examples cited above), the need for love is associated with the pain of rejection. Thus, love is construed as the relation between "tormentor" and "victim" (HOW, 129). Elsewhere in the Beckettian canon, love is associated with extreme personal danger whose immediate analogue is the risk of death. Indeed, when reflecting on his sudden terror, the *Texts* narrator confuses love with the threat of murder and then reassures himself of absolute isolation in the Gobi desert—an image recalling Hamm's reference to "a little bit of grit in the middle of the steppe" (END, 36): "And to start with stop palpitating, no one's going to kill you no one's going to love you and no one's going to kill you, perhaps you'll emerge in the high depression of Gobi, you'll feel at home there" (TFN, 86). The linking of love and mortal danger perhaps derives from the child's dependence on parental figures whose inadequate love implies the threat of abandonment: "We let you cry. Then we moved you out of earshot, so that we might sleep in peace" (END, 56).

In *Endgame*, the problem of love ultimately entrains the problem of God. Here the supreme expression of love withheld pertains to the Deity, who refuses to exist even though the plight of those on "earth" (END, 53, 68, 81) sorely requires him: "The bastard! He doesn't exist!" (55). Closer inspection of the hilarious prayer scene will deepen our understanding of the play. According to well-established custom ("Again!"), Hamm instructs Clov and Nagg to join him in prayer: "Let us pray to God" (54). They adopt appropriate "[a]ttitudes of prayer" (55), but after a few moments each desists, "discouraged": "Sweet damn all!" (55). Here prayer entails the expectation of prompt reward for good action, just as Nagg, in a synchronous context, expects the reward that Hamm promised him for listening to his story: "Me sugar-plum!" (54, 55). But as Hamm advises Nagg, in the midst of the prayer scene, "There are no more sugar-plums!" (55). In response, Nagg accepts responsibility for his own disappointment, attributing its cause to his own mistreatment of Hamm during early childhood:

> It's natural. After all I am your father. It's true if it hadn't been me it would have been someone else. But that's no excuse. (Pause.) Turkish Delight, for example, which no longer exists, we all know that, there is nothing in the world I love more. And one day I'll ask you for some, in return for a kindness, and you'll promise it to me. One must live with the times. (Pause.) Whom did you call when

> you were a tiny boy, and were frightened, in the dark? Your mother? No. Me. We let you cry. Then we moved you out of earshot, so that we might sleep in peace. (END, 56)

With extraordinary compression, the prayer scene conflates the unresponsiveness of God to human entreaty with the reciprocal unresponsiveness of father and son. Just as God the Father ("Our Father which art—" [END, 55]) does not answer prayers, so Nagg the father did not answer his son's nocturnal cries nor, in retaliation for paternal abandonment, does Hamm reward his father's "kindness" or good action.[8] Here the economy of the "universe" (46) is interpreted after the model of dysfunctional father–son love. In alternate formulation, in the world of the play familial love has no more reality than God. Yet there is something deeper here. God does not answer because he does not exist. But he does not exist because he is a "bastard"—that is, too uncaring and selfish to exist. According to this illogical theology, the first principle of being is not the existence of God, as in traditional Christian ontology, but the nonexistence of God, which expresses God's indifference and lack of compassion.

These are the originary qualities in the universe of *Endgame*. In the human sphere, they derive from defective parental love and create, in "the solitary child," the need for autonomy: the need, that is, not to need the love that never responds ("I don't need you any more" [END, 79]). The ultimate means of achieving this autonomy—of satisfying "the need never to need" (W, 202)—is recourse to automatism. In this way, the need for love ("Whom did you call when you were a tiny boy, and were frightened, in the dark?" [END, 56]) is transformed into the need for abandonment so that the compensatory mechanism of automatism can take its course. Yet recourse to automatism reduces life to the temporal process of divestiture, where each beginning signifies only the inevitability of running down until the end, again and again. Hence, to live is to disintegrate.

Notes

1. Compare with Kenner: "its most persuasive metaphor, the play itself" (1968, 160). An even more famous metaphor linked with *Endgame* concerns chess. Indeed, as reported by Anthony Cronin and others, Beckett himself, during rehearsal for the 1967 Berlin production of *Endgame* (Endspiel), told one of the actors that Hamm signified the king and that he was "a bad player." See Cronin (1996, 459–60).

2. See Cohn (1980, 42) and Worton (1994, 80). Connor attributes the heap image to Sextus Empiricus (1988, 123). Worton also cites Eubulides of Miletus and "the *sorites* (or heap) paradox in which he proposed that there can be no such thing as a heap of sand, since one grain does not make a heap and adding one grain is never enough to convert a non-heap into a heap" (1994, 80).

3. In a discussion of Robbe-Grillet's interpretation of Beckett, Bruce Morrissette employs a circumlocution for Hamm's absence: "the non-existence of his own presence." See Morrissette (1975, 69).

4. On immanence and becoming, see also Uhlmann (1999, 126).

5. The Beckett play most frequently related by critics to *Proust* is *Krapp's Last Tape*. See Brater (1987, 19); Henning (1988, 144–58); and Erickson (1991, 181–94).

6. Compare, on this point, Jonathan Boulter: "Clov's complaint is that his experience of the world—or his linguistic representation of it—is bound by a language possibly defunct" (1998, 51).

7. According to Hersh Zeifman, Hamm's reference to nocturnal crying derives from one of Baudelaire's *fleurs du mal*. "Tu reclamais le Soir; il descend, le voici" (Zeifman 1999, 260).

8. According to Joseph Smith, who relates Hamm to God, "In *Endgame* God is not dead. He is not permitted death. He is merely profoundly weary of it all but uncertain that he can be done with it" (1991, 199). For a related study, see Wicker (1998, 39–51).

ENOCH BRATER

Beckett's "Beckett": So Many Words for Silence

I.

This essay begins by urging the reader to observe with its author a full moment of silence, as follows:

. . . .
. . . .
. . . .
. . . .
. . . .
. . . .
. . . .
. . . .
. . . .
. . . .

"Something," as Beckett might say—and in fact did say—"is taking its course." But what, exactly? *Silence once broken will never again be whole.*[1]

Now, any number of things might have happened to interrupt the moment of silence this essay has just tried to manufacture for you. Who knows? You may have laughed, or sighed, or burped, even cried out in dismay. A stomach may have grumbled. That is what live, warm bodies do: throats

From *Reflections on Beckett: A Centenary Celebration,* edited by Anna McMullan and S. E. Wilmer, pp. 190–204.

clear, mouths cough, there's sneezing and—who knows?—perhaps (the matter's delicate) even a Beckettian "fart fraught with meaning."[2]

A pager may have rung. A beeper might have gone off. A battery in a hearing aid might have suddenly set off an alarm. Then there's the omnipresent cell phone. The clock ticks. A foot taps. A pencil falls to the ground, or a paper clip, a coin, a slim piece of paper. Is there music in the background? A door slams. Is the American reader chewing gum or—worse still—is "lip lipping lip"?[3] And so on. Such a busy world! This reading space in which you sit or stand or lie, too, is hardly inviolate: sounds from a hallway and a street life beyond may have already fouled this lame and scripted session of sweet silent thought. Above all, literally, there's the treacherous white noise of electric lights. Proust would be very dismayed. And, to top it off, framing "it all,"[4] there may even be the spectacle of you, reading aloud.

As a celebrated European writer of fiction, poetry, and drama (including in this case the plays written for both the live stage and the mechanical media), Beckett is of course well known for the liberties he has taken with such strange texts of silence. He is by no means the first to have done so. The contentious modernist tradition, from Lamartine to Mallarmé, from Proust to Joyce to Pound, from Schoenberg to John Cage and Giorgio Morandi,[5] has been from the start hell-bent on cauterizing stillness in word and image and sound: *so* many words for silence, so *many* words for silence. But perhaps more so than any other writer of his generation, Beckett structures an absence that is fraught with consequence, yielding (when it works) a resonant blank, full of gestural vigor and pungency:

> Past midnight. Never knew such silence. The earth might be uninhabited.[6]

The lone figure in the single-act *Krapp's Last Tape* is only one of many lost ones we will encounter in Beckett's enigmatic repertory of solitary searchers. "Silence and darkness were all I craved," cries his simulacrum in *Play*, this time planted—buried really—in an urn. "Well, I get a certain amount of both. They being one."[7] "Now the day is over, / Night is drawing nigh-igh," intones Krapp as he stares into stage nothingness near the end of his dubious recording session, his performance richly ironizing the lines of a Protestant hymn he can barely remember from his long ago youth: "Shadows—(*coughing, then almost inaudible*)—of the evening / Steal across the sky." The rest—and Beckett will show it to be the much greater part—is silence.

An Irish writer of the mid-twentieth century, Beckett inherits a tradition of the half-light, the gloaming, a liminal world that is always on the verge of being recovered in some unspecified elsewhere halfway between perceived silence and arrested speech—"relieved," as Didi says in *Waiting for Godot*, but at the same timed "appalled."[8] His early writings, in English and in prose, like to intellectualize *vacuum* and theorize *plenum*, as though further Celtic twilights, all passion spent, might be put on some indefinite hold, not quite gone but definitely on Death Row.[9] His novel *Murphy*, published in London by Routledge in 1938, opens with a real "stinger": "The sun shone, having no alternative, on the nothing new." So far so good. But before long the eponymous hero, whose "fourth highest attribute" is said to be silence, is bound naked to a rocking chair, contemplating in his own time and in his own garret space the dizzying vastness of a "superfine chaos" most readers would be tempted to call the void:

> Now the silence above was a different silence, no longer strangled. The silence not of vacuum, but of plenum.[10]

Beckett's imaginative world will not take fire, however, until he agrees to let the silence in, *both* the vacuum *and* the plenum, not making it—whatever "it" is—into something else, "the screaming silence," for example, "of no's knife in yes's wound."[11] And that's what this critic calls, following Hamm's lead in *Endgame*, a real magnifier:

> Who may tell the tale
> of the old man?
> weigh absence in a scale?
> mete want with a span?
> the sum assess
> of the world's woes?
> nothingness
> in words enclose?[12]

Beckett's cautionary lyric from the Addenda to *Watt*, the novel he was writing in English during the period he was trying to elude the Gestapo by hiding out in the south of France, already thematizes the creative dilemma of not-quite-being-there that will shadow Beckett's work over the next four decades. Even earlier than *Watt*, in the famous letter he wrote to his German friend Axel Kaun on July 9, 1937, he begins to speculate on a highly problematic "literature of the unword" that may finally let silence have its authoritative and persuasive say:

> As we cannot eliminate language all at once, we should at least leave nothing undone that might contribute to its falling into disrepute. To

> bore one hole after another in it, until what lurks behind it—be it something or nothing—begins to seep through; I cannot imagine a higher goal for a writer today. Or is literature alone to remain behind in the old lazy ways that have so long ago been abandoned by music and painting? Is there something paralysingly holy in the vicious nature of the word that is not found in the elements of the other arts? Is there any reason why that terrible materiality of the word surface should not be capable of being dissolved, like for example the sound surface, torn by enormous pauses, of Beethoven's seventh Symphony, so that through whole pages we can perceive nothing but a path of sounds suspended in giddy heights, linking unfathomable abysses of silence? An answer is requested.[13]

Building silence into words will become for Beckett a real "teaser," always a question in his "case nought" of vision rather than technique, though the formidable techniques he develops to do so will be everywhere immaculate and precise.[14] In these post-postructuralist days terms like *vision* and *technique* seem to have fallen into hard times, if not downright disrepute, but they are nonetheless the terms Beckett uses to frame Beckett's "Beckett." These are, moreover, the same congratulatory notes he will sound to negotiate a space for his writing in-between a constructed "said" and the ever-elusive "unsaid," then—*mirabile dictu*—in the even wilder territory that separates the "unsaid" from a previously unchartered "ununsaid." So much for the "Art and Con."[15] Erasure has rarely been subjected to the firm pressure of such an arch and heavy and equally deceptive hand. A term like *overdetermined* now seems like some giddy understatement. The same, of course, might be said of Dante.[16]

Beckett's maturity as a writer's writer comes with the composition of *Molloy*, *Malone Dies*, and *The Unnamable*, the three novels he started writing in French in the late 1940s, then translated fairly quickly into English (though it did not seem so at the time). With virtually simultaneous publication on both sides of the Atlantic, the trilogy, as it became known, soon established his credentials as *the* fifties writer, the most remarked-upon practitioner of all that was fractious and hilarious and nouveau in the *nouveau roman*.

In these books Beckett literally writes himself into the void as his heroes, talkers really, rush pell-mell into silence, every story's final destination. Molloy ends up in a ditch, while the tables fatally turn on his could-be clone, aka Jacques Moran, the Frenchified Irishman; Malone dies, or at the very least suffers a cataclysmic novelistic knockout; and what we may have taken for the Unnamable's endless tirade, despite all protests to the contrary, famously stops dead, all gimmicks gone:

> . . . you must go on, I can't go on, you must go on, I'll go on, you must say words, as long as there are any, until they find me, until they say me, strange pain, strange sin, you must go on, perhaps it's done already, perhaps they have said me already, perhaps they have carried me to the threshold of my story, before the door that opens on my story, that would surprise me, if it opens, it will be I, it will be the silence, where I am, I don't know, I'll never know, in the silence you don't know, you must go on, I can't go on, I'll go on.[17]

End stop. So many, many words, only to arrive at silence, which was always already there, waiting for Beckett, at the beginning of his tri-part tale. "After all," as Murphy says, after all is said and done and spoken and written down, "there is nothing like dead silence." Quite. Murphy's words ring true. The novel has proven to be a clumsy vehicle indeed for letting silence speak its text into this lame unwording of the transparent word. There must be other stratagems.

II.

In the interval between the completion of *Malone Dies* and beginning work on *The Unnamable*, Beckett had the idea of writing a play, mostly, as he told Colin Duckworth, as a relaxation, to get away from the awful prose I was writing at the time." "I wrote *Godot*," he noted in 1985, "to come into the light. I needed a habitable space, and I found it on the stage."[18] The shift in genre will have enormous practical consequences; they bear not so much on the metaphoric representation of silence as on its actual evolution into a highly choreographed performance space. In the theater Beckett will make silence toe the line. Stage directions like *pause*, *brief tableau*, and *Waiting for Godot*'s unforgettable terminus ad quem, "*They do not move*," will freeze the action, letting silence hold the stage with authority, sometimes even poignancy. Ellipsis, as in Winnie's bravura exploitation of this device in *Happy Days*, allows silence, now palpable and theatrically real, to punctuate, formalize, advance, even dictate the direction of the multiple resonances built through nuance into her richly intercalated monologue. Here, too, an embedded *pause* will quite literally allow silence to perform itself, reversing our normal expectations for the conventional relationship between text and subtext. Expanding the moment and arresting the action, silence chastens and conditions dialogue until, beaten into something like submission, it reappears in a rhythm of return, tail, so to speak, between its legs. Mime, as in Clov's spectacular "opener" in *Endgame*, extends the moment even further. Now playing a duet with the lead, silence musicalizes Clov's physical action, clarifying and elevating the complicity of movement in the communication of all stage meaning. Silence, *so to speak*, has suddenly upstaged the provenance of the word.

That is not to say that Beckett's trilogy fiction, so far as silence is concerned, is not without its considerable charms. Although the dual struggle to *be* silent and to let silence *be* is always getting caught in its own delirious traps—and particularly memorable are the ones it sets now deliberately, now inadvertently for itself (as in the humdinger, "I am obliged to speak. I shall never be silent. Never.")—such "idle talk" is nevertheless heard, as fiction generally is, in silence (unless we assume that this outlaw fiction is designed to be read fully and completely out loud, as the actor Barry McGovern has done, a point to consider later in this essay). In *Watt* Beckett tried to describe this phenomenon as something like "a disquieting sound, that of soliloquy, under dictation."[19] But such a mechanism, clever though it is, will not hold still. The very act of saying "silence" makes it far from "absolute," as all three texts in the trilogy are quick to acknowledge. This unnamable subject that both spurns and desires a name sure runs into problems here (*celui-ci*)—as well as there (*celui-là*). The speaker speaking this speech before long finds himself, in spite of himself, narrativizing and thematizing like crazy. And yet "the real silence" is supposed to—and for once in a way let's agree to split the infinitive—only and elegantly *be*.

What a lot of words this trilogy will use to talk instead *around* the subject, if indeed there is (only) one. The so-called silence is at various times alleged to be "little," then "tiny," then "unbroken," then "black," then "immaculate," then "grey," then "perfect," then "comparative" (there's a good one), then "outside," then "inside," then "long," "true," "the same," "murmurous," "short," "absolute," "profound," "different," and "strangled" (my list is not complete).[20] In this ruinous catalog every word is "very rightly wrong," both "ill seen" and "ill said."[21] And each is fated to be equally metonymic, for each can only render up a small part of some unobtainable (w)hole. Undaunted, the emerging word-horde (in various places referenced as "wordshit")[22] holds out the hope of a miraculous "dream silence" and—get this—a "silent silence." Can it be that fiction itself is running out of adjectives—or rather that it "dare not be silent for long, the whole fabrication might collapse"? The inscripted silence that cannot be described is also "prohibited"; on the one hand the text is "condemned to silence," but then on the other hand it has a so-said "right" to it. On "the brink of silence" there are, suggestively,

1. "confines of silence"
2. "drops of silence"
3. "an instant of silence"
4. "a second of silence"

Though "not one person in a hundred knows how to be silent," *things*—and in Beckett there is nothing like things—will be rumored to be mysteriously silent: the dust, various objects, the grave, "my last abode." "To restore silence" is in fact "the role of objects." At times such equivocal silence can only be captured in metaphor or simile, as in "the faint sound of aerial surf." Beckett's narrator "yelp[s]" against such flights of fancy "in vain," for, as he says, "that's the worst, to speak of silence." He longs to "enter living into silence," but then again he has to admit that there's "something gone wrong" with it; "it can never be known." So many words bring the speaker and this speech (not to mention every reader of the trilogy) "not a syllable nearer silence." The fundamentalist taxonomy has been a fraud, a complete waste of time. So, finally, "to hell with silence."

But then, again, when and where the reader least expects to find it, "silence falls with rhetorical intent." There is at long last at the conclusion of this trilogy the blissful finitude of a signature ellipsis, that silent place where the *what* and the *where* of any fiction must end: ". . . . ."

> That is all.
> Make sense who may.
> I switch off.[23]

III.

Beckett's formalist concern—for that is how it is—with the evocation of silence will get a new lease on life once he turns his attention to the stage—and in ways that may have surprised even himself. For in the theater Beckett will be free to explore the mediation of *silence*, *pause*, and *pacing* as economical and efficient grace notes, attenuated time signatures establishing both movement and meaning. When the poor player struts and frets his hour upon Beckett's stage, as on any other, this certainly can signify a whole lot more than nothing. Let us think for a moment of Shakespeare, always a reliable but problematic repertory when it comes to figuring out just where silence is supposed to fall. Shakespeare's script will be hard to quantify here. But that should not indicate that in performance the text must necessarily surrender itself to a director's sometimes heavy hand. When, for example (and as Malone says, "there is nothing like examples"), Othello is about to kill Desdemona in V.ii.7, Shakespeare gives him a curiously suspended line:

> Put out the light, and then put out the light . . .

What is this line supposed to mean? Punctuation, in this case a marked caesura, calls the reader's attention to a pause that must break the line. What the caesura tells us is that we must not in any case recite the line, staccato, like this:

> Put-out-the-light-and-then-put-out-the-light . . .

In this line the caesura is, among other things, the guarantor of metaphor: without silence there will be no meaning here. As always in textual studies of Shakespeare, meaning determines sound; but from the line's point of view it is really the other way around.[24] Just how long does this silence want itself to *be*? And of course there can be no pause here unless it is surrounded and shaped by the sound of Shakespeare's language, a rich "farrago" indeed "of silence and words."[25]

This "pell-mell babel of silence and words"[26] presents us in *Macbeth* with still other problems. In this play an even shorter line can speak volumes, as when Lady Macbeth responds to her husband's hesitation at executing the bloody regicide at hand. "If we should fail?" he cries out in I.vii.59. She completes the broken pentameter line with two well-chosen words:

> We fail?

What roles does silence want to play here in establishing the dynamics of potential meaning in the line? Is it, among other possibilities, *We? Fail?* or is it, rather, the upended shrug of *We fail!* Caesura will not be of the slightest use to us in this instance; and that punctuating question mark has proven to be a deceptive tool before, as in Hamlet's

> . . . O my prophetic soul!
> My uncle?
> (I.v.40–41)

Could it be that these lines yearn to achieve, for strictly characterological reasons, quite a different sound, as follows:

> . . . O my prophetic soul!
> My uncle!

In *Othello* (I.i.118) even an unmarked caesura can authorize the value of silence in advancing the "speaking" of the line. When Brabantio calls Iago a "villain" in the first act of the play, the supersubtle Venetian quickly reacts by giving Desdemona's father his appropriate honorific. Their heated conversation is poised to go something like this, as Iago permutes Brabantio's angry and patrician "thou" to the icy civility of a class-conscious "you." Consider for a moment the very particular interpolation below:

Brabantio. Thou art a villain.
Iago. You are [. . . (*pause*) . . .] a senator.

Beckett's dramaturgy will be highly informed by interventions like these. For as his repertory develops and matures, so do his framing devices for the playing of silence. In the theater, as in music, there will be no silence unless it finds a place for itself in the parenthesis that exists between the sound of other sounds. Lines recited on stage are in this respect both violators and interpreters of silence; in their delay and in their hesitation, in their absence as much as in their presence, they mark silence, ironically, as acutely "real." On stage, as Beckett has shown, following the path of master playwrights like Strindberg, Maeterlinck, and especially Chekhov, silence becomes a highly accomplished ventriloquist, capable of "speaking" for itself in many different tongues. It need no longer rely on a steady stream of questionable adjectives only to say that it is really something else. Words, Beckett's words, "enough to exterminate a regiment of dragoons," have been everywhere calculated on "the Board" to make silence dramatically happen.[27]

Beckett's increasing sensitivity to their volubility can be traced not only in the printed directions for their delivery, an annotation that deepens and expands as the actor moves from *Godot* to *Endgame* to *Happy Days* to *Not I* and beyond, but even more so in the production notebooks the playwright, serving as his own director, kept for the stagings he supervised in London, Stuttgart, and Berlin.[28] This option simply does not exist in the case of Shakespeare (though it does exist to a certain extent in staging Brecht). Words in set repertory with silence and pause, as we have already seen in *Endgame* and *Happy Days*, will not be the only vehicles through which the sound of Beckett's "Beckett" discovers its weight and volume, making itself heard. In the plays he wrote in the 1970s and 1980s, dialogue in the form of soliloquy and monologue will often be overwhelmed by the steady reliance on a far more comprehensive theatrical soundscape, revealing an unexpected urgency where time becomes negotiable in terms of stage space. Here technology, most particularly in the form of the modulation accomplished through sophisticated electronic amplification, will be called upon to play its reciprocal part: chimes, heavy breathing, footfalls, the rocking of a chair, the knocking of a hand on a plain deal table, the closing of a book, or the notation a pencil makes on a notepad will establish and sustain the tonal quality appropriate for each new mise-en-scène. It will be lighting, however, rather than sound, surprisingly, that clarifies mood and atmosphere in this late style, even and especially when the space reveals, as it does in *Rockaby*, a seated figure whose few words—"More"—play a stunning duet with an offstage voice previously recorded on tape, now broadcast as from some unspecified elsewhere.[29] In these short, complex plays, "that MINE,"[30] Beckett's image-making is at full stretch, tacitly admitting the enigma of light as it slowly fades to isolate, diminish, marginalize, fix, and conceal. Such silence is well-spoken indeed.

IV.

In the mechanical media Beckett's staging of silence will become ever more mathematical and precise, sometimes calibrated to the micromillisecond and "every mute micromillisyllable."[31] Here the coefficients can be splendidly timed but also anecdotal, as in the twenty-one-minute "comic and unreal" *Film*, directed by Alan Schneider, where the closeup on a woman's "sssh!" as her finger crosses her lips simultaneously repudiates and intensifies the palpable sound of this black-and-white movie's otherwise silent soundtrack.[32] With the playwright's move to television, the drama in the machine stylizes technology one step further, offering the viewer uninterrupted access to the details of its own heady composition. In plays like *Ghost Trio*, *. . . but the clouds . . .* , and *Nacht und Träume*, Beckett finds a new vocabulary for silence, one primarily designed to suspend the moment for the digitally oriented. Structuring silence and letting it play in black and white and "shades of the colour grey,"[33] Beckett fictionalizes its enterprise and makes us wonder what happens to it as it crosses electronic borders. Recorded music fills in the gaps, surrounding and shaping words but also lending silence body, texture, and, above all, volume. Silence never "acted" quite like this before, Schubert and Beethoven notwithstanding. In *. . . but the clouds . . .* Beckett even makes us hear in silence as the transparency of a woman's face is deftly edited into the frame; when she lingers there in close-up soft focus, she mouths but does not speak the haunting closing lines of Yeats's "The Tower," which we (and then the male voice-over) start to complete for her:

> *W's lips move, uttering inaudibly*: " . . . clouds . . . but the clouds . . . of the sky . . . ," V *murmuring, synchronous with lips*: " . . . but the clouds . . ." *Lips cease. 5 seconds.*[34]

Mallarmé would be pleased; for it was, as he said, only in silence that music might finally achieve its ideal fulfillment.[35]

No one who reads Beckett closely and sympathetically will fail to notice the details of his radiophonic sensibility. His is a full and complete grammar of listening. In his work for the BBC Radio Drama Division with Martin Esslin and Barbara Bray,[36] he ponders the aesthetics of the medium at the same time that he exploits it for practical advantage. In this electronic medium of pure sound, Beckett's vocabulary can become truly bizarre:

> Do you find anything . . . bizarre about my way of speaking? (*Pause.*) I do not mean the voice. (*Pause.*) No, I mean the words. (*Pause. More to herself.*) I use none but the simplest words, I hope, and yet I sometimes find my way of speaking very . . . bizarre. (*Pause.*)[37]

So sounds Maddy Rooney née Donne, the "big pale blur," a formidable woman who must "sound" fat just as her husband Dan must "sound" blind. She quivers like a "blanc mange" and wonders whether her "cretonne" is so unbecoming that she "merge[s] into the masonry." She is also the first of Beckett's destabilizers whose speech intrudes upon the organized presence of radiophonic white noise. On these soundtracks, silence will be both purposeful and percussive as it shapes into being the beat and tempo of an imagined world that insists on getting itself heard. "I open . . . And I close," intones a disembodied voice in the well-named *Cascando*; and "I have come to listen," says a shadowy character named She in *Rough for Radio I.*[38] Rather than hold it at bay, each voice distorts, vitalizes, and animates silence, rendering it whole, giving it body and texture, making us hear the sound of *sound* as if for the first and only time—and for the last time, too, before it fades once more into the void. "Joyce was a synthesizer," Beckett shrewdly observed. "I am an analyzer."[39]

V.

Beckett's groundbreaking late fiction introduces us to the verbal equivalent of solitude, a mysterious atmosphere everywhere empowered by the new lines for "recited" silence previously authorized in the dramas written for the mechanical media where, as he has shown, it knows full well how to pull the pin from the grenade. Especially in the first two volumes of a second trilogy comprising *Company*, *Ill Seen Ill Said*, and *Worstward Ho*, "silence" and "stillness" demand to be read aloud, since much of their emotional resonance lodges in their tonality. In these lyrical works, as in the three-part *Stirrings Still*, the imperatives of silence, literally crying out loud, seek the sound of a human voice, a "helping hand,"[40] in order to formalize and elucidate the stubborn stillness of the universe. Now hear this:

> From where she lies she sees Venus rise. On. From where she lies when the skies are clear she sees Venus rise followed by the sun. Then she rails at the source of all life. On. At evening when the skies are clear she savours its star's revenge. At the other window.

> Rigid upright on her old chair she watches for the radiant one. Her old deal spindlebacked kitchen chair. It emerges from out the last rays and sinking ever brighter is engulfed in its turn. On. She sits on erect and rigid in the deepening gloom. Such helplessness to move she cannot help.[41]

VI.

Wordsworth was lucky. When, in book 1 of *The Prelude*, in a celebrated autobiographical passage, the young poet fixes his "view / Upon the summit of a craggy ridge" and sees the mountain looming beyond, to the very "horizon's utmost boundary," he opens his imagination and his canon to the power and the wonder, the mystery and the silence all around him.[42] Beckett's triumph over stillness (if indeed it is one) will be far "less Wordsworthy."[43] But it will be no less vexed, no less tentative, no less suspect, no less "real," no less intuitive and no less seductive. A contemplative for sure, Beckett is, in this respect, like one of his own early bums, something of a "dud mystic," though he is far from being a full-fledged romantic: no "mystique raté," he just wants to find his text's final word.[44] "Got it at last, my legend." And *what is the word?*[45] Let us listen to it again:

. . . .
. . . .
. . . .
. . . .
. . . .
. . . .
. . . .
. . . .
. . . .
. . . .

After Beckett's "Beckett" and his so *many* words for silence, "so many words for silence" will never sound

. . . .

quite the same again.

Notes

1. Samuel Beckett, *Endgame* (New York: Grove Press, 1958), 32; and *The Unnamable* (New York: Grove Press, 1958), 110.
2. Samuel Beckett, *How It Is* (New York: Grove Press, 1964), 26.

3. Samuel Beckett, *A Piece of Monologue*, in *The Collected Shorter Plays of Samuel Beckett* (New York: Grove Press, 1984), 268.

4. Samuel Beckett, *Footfalls*, in *Collected Shorter Plays*, 240–43.

5. See Richard Begam, *Samuel Beckett and the End of Modernity* (Stanford: Stanford University Press, 1996); and H. Porter Abbott, "Late Modernism: Samuel Beckett and the Art of the Oeuvre," in *Around the Absurd: Essays on Modern and Postmodern Drama*, ed. Enoch Brater and Ruby Cohn (Ann Arbor: University of Michigan Press, 1990), 73–96. See also John Cage, *Silence: Lectures and Writings* (Middletown, Conn.: Wesleyan University Press, 1961).

6. Samuel Beckett, *Krapp's Last Tape*, in *Collected Shorter Plays*, 63.

7. Samuel Beckett, *Play*, in *Collected Shorter Plays*, 156.

8. Samuel Beckett, *Waiting for Godot* (New York: Grove Press, 1954), 8.

9. See John Banville, *The Sea* (London: Picador, 2005), 129.

10. Samuel Beckett, *Murphy* (New York: Grove Press, 1957), 148.

11. Samuel Beckett, *Stories and Texts for Nothing* (New York: Grove Press, 1967), 139.

12. Samuel Beckett, *Watt* (New York: Grove Press, 1959), 247.

13. See Samuel Beckett, *Disjecta: Miscellaneous Writings and a Dramatic Fragment*, ed. Ruby Cohn (London: John Calder, 1983), 51–54, 170–73.

14. Samuel Beckett. . . . *but the clouds* . . . , in *Collected Shorter Plays*, 261; and *Watt*, 147.

15. For the "unsaid" and the "ununsaid," see in particular Samuel Beckett, *Ill Seen Ill Said* (New York: Grove Press, 1981); and *Worstward Ho* (New York: Grove Press, 1983). See also *Watt*, 101.

16. See Daniela Caselli, *Beckett's Dantes: Intertextuality in the Fiction and Criticism* (Manchester: Manchester University Press, 2005).

17. *The Unnamable*, 179.

18. See Enoch Brater, *The Essential Samuel Beckett* (London: Thames and Hudson, 2003), 55.

19. *Watt*, 237. *Molloy*, *Malone Dies* and *The Unnamable*, read by Barry McGovern, were recorded in their entirety and produced for RTE Radio in 2006 by Tim Lehane at The Base, Dublin.

20. For the numerous adjectives modifying *silence* in the trilogy, see *A KWIC Concordance to Samuel Beckett's Trilogy: "Molloy," "Malone Dies," and "The Unnamable,"* vol. 2, ed. Michèle Aina Barale and Rubin Rabinovitz (New York: Garland, 1988), 830–33.

21. Samuel Beckett, Molloy (New York: Grove Press, 1955), 41; and *Ill Seen Ill Said*, for example, 48.

22. *Stories and Texts for Nothing*, 118.

23. Samuel Beckett, *What Where*, in *Collected Shorter Plays*, 316.

24. See Cicely Berry, *The Actor and His Text* (London: Harrap, 1973).

25. *Stories and Texts for Nothing*, 10.

26. *Stories and Texts for Nothing*, 10.

27. *The Unnamable*, 20; *Waiting for Godot*, 55b.

28. See *The Theatrical Notebooks of Samuel Beckett, vols.* 1–4, ed. James Knowlson (London: Faber and Faber, 1993–99). See also Knowlson's *'Happy Days': Samuel Beckett's Production Notebook* (New York: Grove Press, 1985).

29. Samuel Beckett, *Rockaby*, in *Collected Shorter Plays*, 275–80.

30. . . . *but the clouds* . . . , 261.

31. *Stories and Texts for Nothing*, 139.

32. Samuel Beckett, *Film*, in *Collected Shorter Plays*, 163, 165.

33. Samuel Beckett, *Ghost Trio*, in *Collected Shorter Plays*, 248.

34. . . . *but the clouds* . . . , 261.

35. See Enoch Brater, *Beyond Minimalism: Beckett's Late Style in the Theater* (New York: Oxford University Press, 1987), 93.

36. See James Knowlson, *Damned to Fame: The Life of Samuel Beckett* (New York: Simon and Schuster, 1996), 385–87, 421, 442–43; and Martin Esslin, *Mediations: Essays on Brecht, Beckett, and the Media* (Baton Rouge: Louisiana State University Press, 1980), 125–54. See also Bernard Beckerman, "Beckett and the Act of Listening," in *Beckett at 80/Beckett in Context*, ed. Enoch Brater (New York: Oxford University Press, 1986), 149–67.

37. Samuel Beckett, *All That Fall*, in *Collected Shorter Plays*, 13.

38. Samuel Beckett, *Cascando* and *Rough for Radio I*, in *Collected Shorter Plays*, 107, 137.

39. Quoted by Brater, *Beyond Minimalism*, 5.

40. See *Stories and Texts for Nothing*, 55; and *All That Fall*, 23. For a discussion of this point, see Enoch Brater, *The Drama in the Text: Beckett's Late Fiction*. (New York: Oxford University Press, 1994).

41. *Ill Seen Ill Said*, 7.

42. William Wordsworth, *The Prelude*, book I, ll. 369–71; see *English Romantic Writers*, ed. David Perkins (New York: Harcourt, Brace and World, 1967), 217.

43. *Murphy*, 106.

44. A "dud mystic" is the term Belacqua uses to announce the presence of a fictional "Mr. Beckett." He "meant mystique raté, but shrank always from the mot juste." See Samuel Beckett, *Dream of Fair to Middling Women* (Dublin: Black Cat Press, 1992), 186.

45. Samuel Beckett, *Malone Dies* (New York: Grove Press, 1956), 51; and *As the Story Was Told* (London: John Calder, 1990), 131–34.

MATTHEW DAVIES

"Someone is looking at me still": The Audience-Creature Relationship in the Theater Plays of Samuel Beckett

SECK: Unique, oblique, bleak experience, in other words, and would have had same effect if half the words *were* other words. Or any words. (*Pause.*)
SLAMM: Don't stop. You're boring me.
SECK: Not enough. You're smiling.

(Kenneth Tynan 234)

Though Kenneth Tynan was a self-declared "*godotista*" (161), his skit-review of *Endgame* and *Krapp's Last Tape* for the *Sunday Times* in 1958 articulated what has become received wisdom: whatever their literary merits, Beckett's "dramatic vacuums" (159) are difficult for audiences to digest. From his earliest full-length texts with the power to confound or to "claw"[1] through the increasingly eviscerated *dramaticules* delivered at often incomprehensible tempos—rapid (*Play, Not I*), slow (*Footfalls*), or hardly at all (*Breath*)—and culminating in *What Where*'s "Make sense who may. I switch off" (504),[2] Beckett's dramaturgy of developing "impoverishment" approaches a "zero degree theater" (Duckworth 45) that seems "to be an assault on itself, an assault on theater" (Gontarski xvi), an assault on the audience that sustains it.

Yet in spite of Beckett's "pivotal" role in this "tradition of sometimes disdainful sometimes disconcerted ambivalence toward the audience" (Blau

From *Texas Studies in Literature and Language* 51, no. 1 (Spring 2009): 76–93.

34), his works were embraced by large sections of the public from the outset. *Godot*'s 1952 premiere ran for over three hundred performances in Paris and, with *Endgame*, "enjoyed enormous success in Europe" (Tynan 160) before reaching England or America. Over the following decades every addition to the canon was greeted by the swelling ranks of Beckett's "adoring congregation" (Blau 32). His assertion that, done his way, *Godot* "would empty the theater" (Knowlson 379), seems as contradictory as it is self-defeating. As Blau writes, "The more synoptic and extrusive [the plays], the more there is a sense of playing into a void, all the more when there is an audience . . . in respectful or even ritualistic attendance" (34). Clearly the relationship between Beckett's "creatures of illusion on stage" and the audience is, in Duckworth's understatement, "a confused one" (49). The playwright seems to have discovered "a new type of audience/stage transaction that does not fit either side of the traditional Stanislavsky/Brecht dichotomy" (Kalb 39). In this essay I will explore the nature and development of this new transaction.

Though constantly vexed, the relationship between Beckett's creatures of illusion and the audience altered over the course of a career that spanned four decades. I conceive this development in three chronological movements corresponding to Beckett's exploitation of the relations between the auditorium and the stage. The "proscenium arch" plays (*Waiting for Godot*, *Endgame*, *Happy Days*, and the transitional *Krapp's Last Tape*) have fixed, if increasingly indefinable, settings. In the "elliptical light" dramaticules (*Play*, *Not I*, *Footfalls*, *Come and Go*, . . . "but" the clouds . . .) location disintegrates into pools of light surrounded by an encroaching offstage darkness. Finally, in a small but significant pair of metatheatrical plays (*Catastrophe* and *What Where*) Beckett diverts or explodes the pools, forcing the light back into the auditorium and ultimately extinguishing the stage. Such categories are neither neat nor firm, and bleeding occurs across boundaries and time-lines. Yet, these movements suggest three veins of inquiry, each embedded in its appropriate substratum: the relationship between the audience and the onstage characters, the interaction between the audience and the offstage world of the play, and how that relationship mutates when the auditorium becomes host to the playmakers.

I

It might seem misleading to apply the term "proscenium arch" to Beckett's early plays, many of which were designed for, and began life in, studio theaters. Nevertheless, photographic evidence and Beckett's own stage directions demonstrate the requirement for traditional theater architecture[3]—wings (*Godot*), flats with a door and windows (*Endgame*), raised stages (*Krapp*), footlights (*Play*), curtains (*Not I*)—that distances the audience from the stage in a relatively conventional pursuit of sustained theatrical illusion. Throughout his early period Beckett experimented within inherited theater practice. He hugged the walls of his atrophied *theatrum mundi*, exploring the limitations of his environment, testing for chinks in an armor that ultimately proves to be "all chink" (Tynan 159).

To express the sense of developing atrophy, Beckett made metaphors of his stages. In *Endgame*, he dead-ends *Godot's* open road that had promised the tramps at least a modicum of freedom, enclosing the theatrical wings with a grey box set that is hermetically sealed save for two high windows on the back wall and a downstage door to the kitchen, an unwelcoming exterior: "Outside of here it's death" (*Endgame* 97). *Happy Days*, on the other hand, visualizes an unremittingly positive image that contrasts with *Krapp's* negative impression. Krapp's den is a treacherously underlit terrain of banana skins, scrawled ledgers and, later, spool boxes to be navigated by the myopic old man. *Happy Days* depicts the opposite: Winnie's tidy bourgeois principles are matched by a set of "*Maximum simplicity and symmetry. Very* pompier trompe l'oeil *backcloth*" (275). Yet the "blazing light" of perpetual day undermines Winnie's propriety by overexposing her voluptuous, aging upper body. Although the division between the audience and the stage remains clearly demarcated, Beckett's early plays already demonstrate a conflict between the convention of sets, wings, and auditoria, and the more radical operation of lighting and sound effects that increasingly came to dominate the onstage and subvert the audience's sense of place and function.

Denied front doors to suburban streets or French windows onto manicured lawns, Beckett's confined and increasingly immobilized characters find ways to fill that space between now and death: *Waiting for Godot*, narrating the chronicle of their days (*Endgame*) replaying that moment with "my face in her breasts and my hands on her" (*Krapp* 227), talking incessantly in "the old style" to avoid doing "something for a change" (*Happy Days* 293). They pass the time of day "just as we, the audience, pass the time of night," an activity that for Tynan distills the essence of drama into "a means of spending two hours in the dark without getting bored" (159). Not everyone sat around long enough to get bored, however. As Peter Bull, the original English Pozzo, recalls, it did not take long for certain viewers to exercise their ultimate sanction: "Waves of hostility came whirling over the footlights, and the mass exodus, which was to form such a feature of the run of [*Godot*], started quite soon after the curtain had risen" (Knowlson 414). The bewilderment, exasperation, even anger, inherent in such actions suggests that, despite a rapidly developing audience, some spectators felt they were being duped, conned. While Parisians accustomed to "the alluvium of the absurd" (Blau 43) embraced Beckett, he proved far more baffling to an "English theater that had been dominated for half a century by George Bernard Shaw" (Henderson and Oliphant 48), since he resolutely denied the kind of intellectual interpretations that would satisfy a predominantly middle-class, educated audience. "Why people have to complicate a thing so simple I can't make out," Beckett responded bluntly to the various interpretations of *Godot*, offered in the English press (Knowlson 375).

Yet Beckett's evasion of the audience's "craze for explicitation" (*Catastrophe* 487) seems somewhat disingenuous. His long plays contain traditional literary and dramatic qualities—recognizable characters, cultural allusions that suggest inherent significance, hints of plot and past lives, mutable relationships expressed through cross-talk and verbal gymnastics—that do more than suggest interpretation or emotional association: they demand it. Like the tree, the carafe, and the rope lowered from the flies in *Act Without Words I*, meaning and empathy are repeatedly dangled before the audience, violently withdrawn at the command of an offstage whistle, then dangled once more—a frustrating cycle of *cogitatio interrupta*. Beckett's technique of stroboscopic significance makes of his texts a mosaic of broken or incomplete metaphors and mythologies that defy interpretation, baffling audience and performer alike: "*Hamm*. We're not beginning to . . . to . . . mean something? *Clov*. Mean something! You and I, mean something! [*Brief laugh*.] Ah, that's a good one!" (*Endgame* 115). The texts demand interpretation precisely to show the futility of interpretation. The audience's teleological impulse is a reenactment of what is enacted on stage, the vain, if entirely human, struggle to "create a little order" in a senseless universe: "Ah the creatures, the creatures. Everything has to be explained to them" (*Endgame* 122).

Should the audience be reluctant to concede its participation in Beckett's futile universe, and seek instead to hide in the safety of the anonymous auditorium, the onstage characters occasionally reach out across the footlights as if momentarily sensing our presence. At critical moments in his long plays, Beckett creates hairline fractures, chinks in the fourth wall that confuse the boundary between representation and reality: "*Estragon*: Charming spot. [*He turns, advances to front, halts facing auditorium*.] Inspiring prospects. [*He turns to Vladimir*.] Let's go" (*Godot* 8). Often comic, these schisms are also accusatory, discomforting. After experiencing the "strange feeling that someone is looking at me," Winnie recalls, "Mr. and Mrs. Shower . . .—or Cooker" (names Beckett derived from German words referring to looking, spectating[4]), who have come to stare at and critique her: "What's the idea? he says—stuck up to her diddies in the bleeding ground" (*Happy Days* 293–94). Having thus far directed her monologue at the mound, the "zenith," and Willie's rear, the usually benign Winnie quite suddenly "[*raises head, gazes front*.] And you, she says, what's the idea of you, she says, what are you meant to mean?" (*Happy Days* 294). Is Winnie reiterating Mrs. Shower's attack on her husband? Or are Mr. and Mrs. Shower synechdochal figures for the audience? Prefiguring the narrative switch to third person adopted by Mouth in *Not I* and May in *Footfalls*, Winnie's derision makes the audience painfully self-conscious and uncertain of its function. Its gaze briefly inverted, the watchers become watched, though too remotely to allow us a shred of narcissistic pleasure. In a period dominated by naturalistic theater and an adherence to the suspension of disbelief, Beckett's assaults on the fourth wall create metatheatrical fractures that undermine the egotistical nature of performance *and* spectating.

The "immaterialist" philosophy of the eighteenth-century Bishop Berkeley—*esse est percipi*—lies at the heart of Beckett's dramatic conception of the performative self. The shaping conceit in Beckett's screenplay, *Film* (1965), this Berkeleyan concept underpins most of Beckett's theatrical works, for all his characters must be perceived to exist, and they must perform to be perceived: "I act therefore I am," or, "I do not act therefore I am not (or, no more)." Beckett's characters are all actors by necessity, their existence is theater: "this farce day after day" (*Endgame* 14); an "audition" for "my last soliloquy" (*Endgame* 77). They perform pratfalls and comedy routines with hats, songs, and stories, social activities that Alan Friedman calls "party pieces."[5] Mostly they just talk: "*Clov.* What is there to keep me here? *Hamm.* The dialogue" (*Endgame* 135). Driving the dialogue is the characters' terror that they are becoming invisible, unattended; that, in Beckett's words, silence is pouring into their diminishing existence "like water into a sinking ship" (Graver 24). Vladimir registers his fear to the Boy in *Godot*: "Tell him . . . [*he hesitates*] . . . tell him you saw us. [*Pause.*] You did see us, didn't you? *Boy.* Yes Sir" (45). Faltering perception is registered through hearing as well as sight: "*Nagg.* Can you hear me? *Nell.* Yes. And you? *Nagg.* Yes. [*Pause.*] Our hearing hasn't failed. *Nell.* Our what? *Nagg.* Our hearing. *Nell.* No" (*Endgame* 102). And as responses diminish, merely the perception of being perceived suffices: "just to know in theory that you can hear me even though in fact you don't, is all I need" (*Happy Days* 285). Increasingly, Beckett's characters act not for us but for themselves; they are performing for their lives.

Yet herein lies the existential crisis for the audience, for while we do hear and see the performers, they rarely perceive us, recognize our participation. Kalb describes Beckett's double-acts as clowns whose "jokes and gags may be perfectly executed yet not provoke laughs" (29). Onstage spectators largely ignore, reject, or disdain requests for attention. Hamm has to bribe his father with a bonbon to listen to his life story, while Nagg's "tailor's joke" receives only his wife's blank expression: "It's not funny" (*Endgame* 106). Their momentary sensations that, in Winnie's words, "Someone is looking at me still" (*Happy Days* 299), painfully underscore our failure to fulfill our side of the transaction: *we*, the perceivers, are unable to meet the performers' needs.

We laugh at Nagg's tailor joke, but he cannot hear our laughter, and he measures his fatal decline accordingly: "I tell this story worse and worse" (*Endgame* 22). Our introjective function frustrated, we become redundant voyeurs, our unresponsiveness making us complicit in Nagg's death.

The audience feels as neglected, or rejected, as the onstage characters. Beckett creates of his fourth wall a two-way mirror through which his performers, desperate for "Eyes on my eyes" (*Happy Days* 299), enact their solitude. Like all actors, when they stare into the auditorium, they discern only darkness—Krapp is shortsighted, Hamm blind, Clov sees only a reflection of his own "light dying"—with merely the residue of an offstage presence. Hamm throws the whistle toward the auditorium "with my compliments" (*Endgame* 154), but it doesn't get there. Krapp kicks his banana skin off the stage into "*the pit*" (*Krapp* 222), no further. When Clov turns his looking glass on "the without," he brings us too close for legibility: "I see . . . a multitude . . . in transports . . . of joy. (*Pause.*) That's what I call a magnifier" (*Endgame* 112). On his ladder, Clov pans between the two upstage windows and the only other available opening, the auditorium. The focus is better, but the view far worse: "Let's see. [*He looks, moving the telescope.*] Zero . . . [*he looks*] . . . zero [*he looks*] and zero. . . . Corpsed" (*Endgame* 112–13). The auditorium is a "charnel house" (*Godot* 57) from which Estragon "*recoils in horror*" (66). We are dead to the stage, redundant. The failure by both sides to make contact is rendered all the more painful by our brief glimpses of missed connections through Beckett's ruptured fourth wall: "*Estragon*. You don't have to look. *Vladimir*. You can't help looking" (*Godot* 57).

Duckworth argues for the impossibility of tragic catharsis in Beckett's "desperately private drama[s]" precisely because of this lack of contact: "the decisive encounter will not occur, in which the conflict will not take place" (95). Yet Beckett creates more than a spectacle, a *chose vue*, from which the spectator remains emotionally detached. In contrast to Brecht and Genet, "there is something beguiling about Beckett's [longer] plays, a seduction in their dying fall, that is as accessible as it is forbidding" (Blau 34). There is a deep well of sadness in the pre-lives of Beckett's early characters, a sense of lost chances and loves; of punts on streams or row boats on Lake Como; of journeying up the Eiffel Tower and down the Ardennes; of "something . . . dripping . . . a heart. A heart in my head" (*Endgame* 97). They are not mean or vicious by nature; they are made so by life: "*Clov*. That's friendship, yes, yes, no question, you've found it. . . . Then one day, suddenly it ends" (*Endgame* 81). In the face of unremittingly tragic farce, they display a pathetic heroism that is deeply empathetic: "*Clov*. There's no more painkiller. *Hamm* (*appalled*). Good . . . ! (*Pause.*) No more painkiller. (*Soft.*) What'll I do?" (*Endgame* 71). Even at the end of the game decorum prevails: "*Clov*. Ah, pardon, it's I am obliged to you. *Hamm*. It's we are obliged to each other" (*Endgame* 81).

That the audience is kept at a distance from Beckett's pathetic farces, forced to watch from the other side of the mirror, validates the bleak honesty of the picture. As Pinter wrote, contrasting Beckett's characters to Brecht's, "they are not selling me anything I don't want to buy" (Kalb 46). Neither side has anything ideological or pedagogical to trade. None of the common devices for crossing the fourth wall are proffered, no asides, nudges, or winks. No boy arrives out of the desert promising salvation. There is no "underplot," just minor calamity suffered by "small men locked in a big space" (Knowlson 435).[6] Arthur Koestler describes this kind of catharsis as "a sense of individual tragedy . . . earthed in man's universal tragedy, personal sorrow dissolved in a vaster feeling" (qtd. in Duckworth 95). In the following two decades, such universal empathy, however futile or bleak, became increasingly eviscerated for Beckett. As stage space conceded to the invading darkness of offstage, language diminished toward silence, characters devolved into creatures, and plays dwindled to *dramaticules*, the possibility of audience empathy would fade (almost) to zero. Yet an audience ignored would become an audience involved, implicated and, ultimately, liberated.

II

Gontarski argues that Beckett's works are all post-*Play* pieces. Taking sole directorial responsibility for the 1973 Berlin Schiller-Theater production of *Play* seems to have instigated in Beckett a process of dramaturgical diminution, of stripping away character, text, and narrative, retrospectively as well as in his future work. He was, in Gontarski's words, "no longer throwing his bricks against naturalism . . . that particular victim was already on life-support, but against modernism itself" (xv). The already pared down style of *Endgame*, which Beckett had described as "elliptical" ("defective, or lacking . . . words" [*OED* 2]), became increasingly formal, patterned, verbally spare, and centered on the Cartesian division of mental consciousness and physical reality. Beckett explored Descartes's mind-body dichotomy on stage through separating action and word: Camera and Joe in the television piece, *Eh Joe*; Eye (E) and Object (O) in *Film*; Mouth and Auditor in *Not I*; May (M) and Woman's Voice (V) in *Footfalls*; W[oman] and V[oice] in *Rockaby*; Reader and Listener in *Ohio Impromptu*. This textual ellipsism seems designed to provoke even greater alienation in an audience scrambling not only for meaning but also for any kind of recognizable human qualities with which to associate or empathize. Destabilizing his audience also allowed Beckett to wield greater control, to impose his authority both on and off stage, even, as in *Play*, to embody himself in the auditorium.

At the same time that Beckett created dehumanized elliptical texts, he also developed a new kind of staging to express the physical entrapment of his increasingly disembodied creatures. Beginning with the prototypical *Krapp*, Beckett replaced sets and a fourth wall with elliptical—or spherical—pools of light, chiaroscurist playing spaces that are delimited, circumscribed, and controlled by directorial forces. Paradoxically, while textual ellipsism pushes the audience away, physical ellipses draw the audience in, for a diminished onstage serves to enlarge the offstage that is sucked into the vacuum. The more compressed the lit area of the performance space, the more dominant the encroaching darkness that surrounds it, including not just backstage, wings, and the "dark aura" of the unlit stage, but the auditorium itself: by definition, spheroids have no sides. The audience's anonymous space becomes part of the performance space, a penumbral anti-stage invading the stage, making the audience inhabitants of Beckett's universe whether we like it or not. What we cannot be sure of is whether this offstage world is inhabited by the living or by the dead, and whether those inhabitants are benevolent or cruel.

In Beckett's universe death, it seems, waits for an age: " . . . what? . . . seventy? . . . good God! . . ." (*Not I* 411). Those in their fifties and sixties—Didi and Gogo, Pozzo, Hamm, Willie—are rapidly approaching death; the prematurely old, like W in *Rockaby*, approach even faster. Those past seventy might already be posthumous: "*M.* What age am I now? . . . *M.* Ninety. / *V.* So much?" (*Footfalls* 428); while those with uncertain ages seem uncertain whether they are alive *or* dead: "*M.* What age am I now? / *V.* In your forties. / *M.* So little?" (428). Krapp, however, knows his age exactly—he has measured out his life with birthday spools—and seems to understand its limit. At sixty-nine he tries, and fails, to record his final tape: "Nothing to say, not a squeak. . . . Go on with this drivel in the morning. Or leave it at that. [*Pause.*] Leave it at that" (*Krapp* 227–28). Beckett told the German actor, Martin Held, "Old Nick's there. Death is standing behind him and unconsciously he's looking for it" (Pilling 82).

Krapp transitions into a series of plays that could, therefore, be termed purgatorial as well as elliptical, with Beckett's creatures approaching, listening at, or passing through, death's door. The shuffling Krapp visiting his offstage kitchen with increasing frequency, first for beer, then spirits, as if absorbing alcohol for the Stygian journey to which he has sacrificed a lifetime's preparation, weaves drunkenly in and out of the darkness, flirting with death. And darkness, or death, is what all Beckett's purgatorial creatures await, or have already experienced, with a craving plagued by contingency: "Dying for the dark—and the darker the worse. Strange" (*Play* 365). In crossing the outer ring of the ellipsis, Krapp comes precariously close both to death and to the audience. Briefly we share the same penumbral space, the same light. It is a convergence that poses an uncomfortable question for the audience: who is walking on whose grave?

By *Footfalls* (1975), Beckett had almost entirely obliterated the division between light and dark, stage and offstage, bringing Clov's vision of the "hell out there" into the whole theater—stage and auditorium: "Gray. Gray! GRRRAY! Light black from pole to pole" (*Endgame* 112). The audience peers voyeuristically through a keyhole, a "chink" that opens onto the stage rather than into the auditorium, as if the light is succumbing to the offstage darkness, succumbing, perhaps, to us. May paces a flattened ellipsis, a corridor squeezed dry of light, measuring her diminishing life cycle over three scenes, until the gloaming rises for a final time on a bare stage that "comes very close to zero" (Cohn 335). Beckett's complex narrative similarly collapses in on itself, blending matter and anti-matter. The mother's voice speaks intermittently through the body of her daughter, Amy, who then tells a tale of May (M), (an anagram of herself), and the fictional girl's mother, Mrs. Winter (Mrs. W), an inversion of M. As Knowlson writes, "We realize . . . that we may have been watching a ghost telling a story of a ghost" (qtd. in Cohn 337). In a denouement that is visually startling and viscerally chilling, the audience relives the moment of death, the point when *Footfalls*'s ellipsis "flatlines," and the corridor is emptied of life. The division between stage and offstage is so faint that M's devoiced body might have drifted into the auditorium, not so much bringing the dead to life as mortifying the living. In contrast to the fatal disconnectivity of the proscenium plays, there is, nonetheless, something bleakly comforting in the convergence of dying characters and dead audience in *Krapp* and *Footfalls*, a sense of communion captured in the resigned defiance of V's valedictory "Fuck life" (*Rockaby* 470). Into the dark liminal spaces of *Play* and *Not I*, however, Beckett introduced shadowy figures that worry the onstage characters and make uneasy alliances with the spectator.

In *Play* a man (M), his wife (W1), and his mistress (W2), heads "*lost to age*" protruding from "*identical grey urns*" (*Play* 355), reiterate the tawdry events of a *ménage à trois* that may have led to murder and/or suicide: "*M.* She had a razor in her vanity bag" (358); "*W2.* I felt like death" (358). Their melodramatic moments of *crise* and *ennui* are spliced together by a "unique inquisitor" (367), who operates a "single mobile spot" on the three speakers. In effect, Beckett diminishes the elliptical performance space to the size of a head and the top of an urn, as each "*victim*" (366) is provoked into response by the brutal, capricious spotlight: "Looking for something. In my face. Some truth. Not even" (366). The interrogation is something upon which all three have become dependent: "*W1.* Is it something I should do with my face, other than utter? . . . *M.* Am I as much as being seen?" (366) They are obliged to speak, rather than told what to say, by a "torturer"[7] whose inhumanity is laid bare: "*W2*. Some day you will tire of me and go out . . . for good. *W1*. Hellish half-light" (361). Beckett stages "a conflict between antithetical desires: to lose the self in darkness and to confront the self in light" (Lyons 101), an antithesis that has metadramatic implications for an audience that, residing anonymously in the "hellish half-light," is compelled to wonder as to which side of the conflict it belongs.

Beckett specifies that the "source of the light . . . must not be situated outside the ideal space (stage) occupied by its victims" (366). The operator, however, cannot share the stage without masking our view of urns that are only "one yard high" (367). That the faces must be lit "at close quarters and from below" (366) suggests that the operator is standing at the foot of the apron—in the auditorium, back clearly visible to an audience that shares "its" space. The inclusion of lighting technician, Duncan M. Scott, in the program for the Royal Court production in 1976 suggests that the spot operator, as well as the light itself, becomes a major, and highly provocative, figure in performance. Does the inquirer stand between the audience and "its" victims, barring our empathetic responses? Or is "it" our representative, "a metaphor for our attention, relentless, all-consuming, whimsical"? (Kenner 141). Are we frightened by its brutality or impressed by its skill? Above all, do we, like Beckett's creatures, need the inquisitor to fulfill our defunct introjective role, to make *Play* play? In situating such a dominating presence between the auditorium and the stage, Beckett provokes fundamental questions about the power struggle inherent in dramatic production between spectator, producer, and performers.

Not I introduces Beckett's most striking, and certainly most realized, presence in the "hellish half-light," the "*Auditor . . . a tall standing figure, sex undeterminable, enveloped from head to foot in loose black djellaba, with hood fully faintly lit*" (405). Downstage, "*audience left*," the figure listens intently as an upstage Mouth, eight feet above the stage and enveloped by darkness, disgorges a logorrhea of broken recollections of her tragic life from premature birth and abandonment, through a trauma-induced muteness (aside from occasional winter outbursts), to a sudden release of words, possibly at the point of her death—the moment which we are now experiencing. Her life literally flashes past her: " . . . dull roar like falls . . . and the beam . . . flickering on and off" (411). Though Mouth's narration militates against audience involvement—she is distant, remote, disembodied, and barely intelligible—the effect of the tightest elliptical stage in the Beckett canon draws us ineluctably to the object of the noise: "We pass through the same stages as she is describing" (Kenner 214).

While critics have noted the Auditor's dramatic impact, its purpose and efficacy are debatable.[8] Schneider wrote to Beckett from rehearsals in

New York: "Figure confuses almost everyone, not location but presence. I find the juxtaposition of two arresting but not really explainable" (162). Beckett acceded to requests to drop the figure from the French premiere in 1975 (an extremely rare move on his part), reinstated it for his own staging three years later, before conceding in 1986 that it might have been "an error of the creative imagination" (Knowlson 617). Watching Billie Whitelaw's reprisal of the Mouth on the small screen in 1977, Beckett realized that the sustained close-up without the Auditor was "far more arresting, sensual, than anything that could be achieved in the theater" (Friedman 163). The stage demise of the Auditor (it has been retained in the text) is significant in demonstrating a developing feature of the elliptical plays: Beckett's growing domination over both his creatures and his audience.

Inherent in the notion of "someone watching the watcher" (Knowlson 161) is the dilemma that the Cartesian division of listener and speaker, intrinsic to Beckett's work, risks being replaced by a more practical problem—split focus. By instigating a three-way dialogue among Viewer, Auditor, and Speaker, Beckett risks releasing the "claw" of his text, thereby letting his audience off the hook. The voyeuristic discomfort of watching a figure listening to a dying cripple describing her sense of guilt for a past sexual experience ("when clearly intended to be having pleasure . . . she was in fact . . . having none" [407]) is perhaps too easily mitigated by our association with the figure's sympathetic gesture "of helpless compassion" (405), the raising and falling of its arms. Replicating Mouth's self-defensive refusal to "relinquish third person" (405)—" . . . what? . . . who? . . . no! . . . she!" (406)—the third-person audience, the plural "we," can too easily abrogate responsibility to the onstage Auditor and retreat into a deeper darkness: "shut out the light . . . reflex they call it . . . no feeling of any kind" (408). If we are compelled, however, to focus on the manifestation of female expression floating hypnotically above our heads, then the receptacle of language begins to resemble a female sexual organ, a "tiny little thing . . . godforsaken hole . . . no love . . . spared that" (411), through whose lips words come rushing forth like titillating tidbits: "a tongue in the mouth . . . all those contortions without which . . . no speech possible" (409). To borrow Friedman's phrase, the audience (rather than the Auditor) "silently insinuates itself inside Mouth's head" (160). We are no longer a "spectator of the anguish but a participant" (Knowlson 214). We become complicit in the interrogation.

In the version of *Not I* stripped of its "figure," Beckett's technique of elliptical staging reaches its zenith. Unlike the early proscenium arch plays that deny the interaction both characters and audience require for self-validation, Beckett's increasingly diminished ellipses work like visual vacuums upon an audience drawn to the diminishing stage light like moths to a dying flame.

The pathetic creatures that inhabit this penumbral space—decrepit, sinister, wraithlike, dismembered—make discomfiting, even alarming, company, working "on the nerves of the audience, not its intellect" (Gontarski xvii).[9] They are not, however, fearful monsters raging at the dying of their light, but pitiful creatures compelled to "revolve" their disappointing lives and their distended deaths by a heartless interrogator emanating from the auditorium with whom we, by virtue of the theatrical setting, are inherently complicit. *Not I* graphically realizes this guilty collusion by contrasting the image of the voluptuous Mouth with the voice of the "old crone" (Knowlson 522)[10] who is seventy years old, the dying age for Beckett's creatures. By generating an almost necrophilic response to Mouth, the audience confronts the truth that Beckett's *dramaticules* play, or make plays upon, the body parts of the dead and the dying, bodies brought into increasingly obscene focus through a series of contracting elliptical lenses.

The inherent voyeurism in Beckett's *dramaticules*, and our participation in it, is neither lubricious nor cruel, but rather the theatrical manifestation of the friction between the artist's existentialism and a dramatic medium "that has caused us since its first humiliated appearance to think about the theater with the most appalling doubt" (Blau 181). If, as Pozzo says and Didi repeats, human existence is giving birth "astride of a grave" (*Godot* 82–83), what story does humanity offer the dramatist but its dying, and where else can an audience view that story but six feet under, looking up? Such a perspective is as honest as it is obscene. In subverting the fourth wall, bringing darkness to the light, and blending both into "Grrey" (*Endgame* 114), Beckett's *dramaticules* collapse the Cartesian division between watcher and watched. Witnesses to the point zero of human existence, the conception of our deaths, we become midwives at our births, mourners at our funerals, participants in our universal anguish. And we have plenty of company.

Since *Godot* first failed to arrive, audiences have wondered who (or what) screams or whistles, holds the goad or rings the bell, guides the light or asks the questions in Beckett's plays. *Not I* depicts this presence in the auditorium as an interrogative light that, unlike in *Play*, derives from a sinister, unseen force emanating from the beam's source. Differentiating itself from *Play*'s capricious "inquisitor," this intangible presence appears to have a purpose, demanding accuracy and absolute obedience: "She did not know . . . what position she was in . . . whether standing . . . or sitting . . . or kneeling . . . but the brain, . . . what? . . kneeling? . . . yes" (*Not I* 406). Mouth directs her ravings, revised and corrected, to a bullying pedant in the darkness. Rather than asking the questions, the Auditor merely responds with a helpless shrug. Billie Whitelaw, who underwent the disorienting ordeal of being suspended, caged, hooded, only her mouth unmuzzled, to perform *Not I*, similarly (if surprisingly fondly) describes Beckett as "very particular and meticulous . . . insist[ing] that it be right" (Friedman 210). The association between the directorial light and Beckett as *auteur*—as "authority of stage as well as page" (Friedman 149)—becomes unavoidable in *Not I*. It is as if Beckett is drawing attention to his own dominating presence in the auditorium; he is making himself known.

III

Self-exposure by such an intensely private artist was slow to be performed. A decade after *Not I*, Beckett wrote two overtly political plays, the first of which, a self-imposed catastrophe that threatened to dismantle not only the theater's conventional fourth wall but Beckett's entire theatrical edifice, would turn his dramaturgy inside out. *Catastrophe*, the centerpiece to "A Night for Vaclav Havel," was first performed at the Avignon Festival in 1982. Havel, political prisoner and future Czech president, was also a renowned playwright, so there is, for Beckett, an uncharacteristic logic to the play's metatheatrical metaphor of the twin tyrannies of dramatist and director. Yet, in staging a rehearsal in which the "*final touches*" are made to the "*last scene*" (485) of an undocumented performance, Beckett seems to be concluding the action of his own personal and professional drama. With *Catastrophe* and *What Where* (1984), he plays out a swift and brutal epilogic endgame to his career; in turning the interrogatory light upon himself he catches the audience in the corona of his self-examination.

As early as *Rough for Theatre I*, which was written in the late fifties, Beckett began assigning reduced nomenclature to his degenerating characters. *Catastrophe*'s abbreviations, however, go beyond the reductive to imply something self-critical, with D variously suggesting the dramatist, dramaturg, director, dictator. Paired with his obedient (A)ssistant, D and A replicate the master–servant genetic code that reaches back to Pozzo and Lucky. The Director's dialogue is dense with politically barbed humor ("Step on it, I have a caucus" [486]), meta-theatrical derision ("This craze for explicitation!" [487]), and, considering the "unbecoming vigilance" (Blau 34) with which Beckett has recorded his own productions, pointed self-mockery: "For God's sake! Every i dotted to death!" (487). A shows traces of humanity: she observes that P is shivering (whether with cold, fear, or anger), but yields instantly to D's commands in the debased language of shorthand: "I make a note" (486). All the while P—protagonist, performer, puppet, political prisoner—stands on an 18-inch dais on the stage like a black-garbed David or a degenerative Hamlet, an actor robbed of his lines. Michael Billington captures the powerfully unadorned metaphor of the work: "the tyranny of the state is combined with the inherent autocracy of the theater . . . dictatorships venerate and persecute artists at the same time" (Beryl and John Fletcher 264). Yet the metatheatrical nature of the work also makes the aesthetic criticism personal.

In a diastolic gesture unique to his *oeuvre*, Beckett returns light to the house to expose the power behind the play. As *Catastrophe* opens, D is discovered in the auditorium, "*in an armchair downstairs audience left. Fur coat. Fur toque to match*" (485). He smokes a large cigar while receiving the ministrations of his attractive assistant. When he quits his seat and retreats to the back of the theater to check for sight lines, we are compelled to shift perspective, to twist in our seats so as to seek out the smallest of all Beckett's ellipses: the tip of D's smoldering cigar. D treats his actor like a creature, barely human: "Take off that gown. . . . Could do with more nudity. . . . Bare the neck. . . . The legs. Higher" (488). Pedantic, voyeuristic, casually lascivious, D poses the same questions and makes demands reminiscent of those to which W1 and Mouth have already responded. Beckett has D embody the interrogatory light of *Play* and *Not I*, which, followed to its source, can have only one name: Beckett.

What Where, Beckett's final play, also depicts the tyrannical director, though he is now a fully separated egotistical force termed V "*in the shape of a small megaphone at head level*" (496). Through the seasons of his existence he demands of four figures (one being himself) the answer to "it," "what," "where," "And where" (500 *et passim*). Each failed interrogator is tortured in turn, until the final figure, *Bem*, offers to give an answer without giving it—presumably because no answer exists. This response does not interest V who, having finally been offered what he has demanded, replies: "Good. I am alone. . . . Time passes. Make sense who may. I switch off" (505). D, in *Catastrophe*, having similarly shaped and carved P into his desired image, declares no interest in the performance: "Good. There's our *Catastrophe*. In the bag. Once more and I'm off" (488). Beckett in effect admits to having manipulated, goaded, tortured, and generally brutalized his performers in his quest for existential answers that do not exist, while placing little or no value on the reception, the product(ion). The exploration, the rehearsal, is everything, the performance nothing. Such anti-theatricality seems to be a critique not of Beckett's actors, who often engage in "acts of silent opposition" (Friedman 175), but of the audience's complicit participation in his activities.

Luke, D's offstage deputy, dims the house lights in *Catastrophe*, creating, for a final time, a diminishing ellipsis that comes to rest on P's head, whereupon P performs a gesture that is as shocking as it is unique: "*P raises his head, fixes the audience*" (489). For the only time in the canon, a Beckett character stares directly at us, "eyes on [our] eyes" (*Happy Days* 299) with a look that is accusatory, chastening, defiant. "There's no ambiguity there at all," Beckett told Knowlson. "He's saying, you bastards, you haven't finished me yet" (598). As the sound system plays a "*Distant storm of applause*" that "falters," then "dies" (*Catastrophe* 489), the audience is left utterly confounded as to the appropriate response. To remain silent would confirm our redundancy as an audience, to applaud would confirm our subservience to the playmaker. We have been perceived for what we are and might always have been in Beckett's theatrical universe: willing pawns in an endless game sustained by our own participation. As Hamm says, staring blindly into the auditorium: "Old stancher! / [Pause.] / You . . . remain" (*Endgame* 154). Politically and aesthetically, *Catastrophe* argues that, without the support of a suppliant audience of adoring acolytes, theaters of torture, like theaters of war, would cease to exist.

Should the audience feel betrayed, even outraged, by Beckett's ultimate repudiation of its function, or concerned that his artistic crisis has reached a critical mass from which there was to be no return? Alternatively, might we feel energized by a political call to arms or wryly amused by the ultimate Beckettian conundrum: theater staging rejection of the theater? Were Beckett asked these questions he would probably, like his shadowy Auditor, shrug his shoulders "in a gesture of helpless compassion" (*Not I* 405). Yet Beckett's slap in the audience's face is hardly a *volte-face*. As we have seen, persistent artistic and philosophical anxieties concerning Beckett's power relations with his actors and his audience were embodied as early as 1969 in *Play*'s inquisitorial light and only fully realized in D thirteen years later. By returning to a conventional dramatic format with *Catastrophe*, Beckett squares the ellipsis of his career, returning, as his narratives always do, to a diminished beginning, achieving in his valediction that which he desired at the inception of *Godot*: an empty auditorium.

On the other hand, *Catastrophe* is Beckett's penultimate rather than final play, and its tone is energetically didactic rather than valedictory. His return to the proscenium format can be read as an iconoclastic gesture, an expansion that collapses his theatrical boundaries as much as it assaults the ideological wall dividing east from west. By bringing light to the auditorium, Beckett converts the failed contacts of his proscenium plays into the full contact of a metatheatrical affront. He switches allegiances rather than "switch[es] off" and "let[s us] have it" (*Catastrophe* 489) between the eyes, the ocular challenge of P shaming us out of the theater and onto the streets. The stare is purposeful. "He'll have them on their feet," D concludes, deaf to the irony. "I can hear it from here" (489). Judging by *Catastrophe*'s artistic, and arguably political, success, P's silent defiance did not fall on deaf ears.

Among Beckett's plays, *Catastrophe* is ultimately, and uniquely, optimistic in the expectations it places on its audience, and the play's didacticism perhaps mitigates for Beckett the persistent paradox that his audience refused to listen to him: they continued to come. *Catastrophe* was a smash hit when it transferred to New York in 1983, and Beckett hailed a "living genius" by the *Times* critic, Frank Rich. When The Samuel Beckett Theater opened on Broadway a year later, *Footfalls* was the "most sought after event of the season" (Knowlson 604). Beckett's audience was swelling, not diminishing. As Schneider wrote, in appropriately otherworldly terms, "All hell is breaking loose" (qtd. in Knowlson 604). Beckett's "dead voices . . . babbling from the Lethe" (*Embers* 201) joined other dissenting speakers to create a clamor heard by alternative audiences, absent, antagonistic, yet seemingly attendant to the message emerging from a theater without walls. While we can only surmise what influence "A Night for Vaclav Havel" exerted on the Czech authorities' decision to release their celebrated dissident in 1983, Havel's subsequent letter to Beckett expressed his personal gratitude to one who "does not give [himself] away in small change. . . . For a long time afterwards there accompanied me in the prison a great joy and emotion that helped [me] to live on amidst all the dirt and baseness" (Knowles 598). Perhaps the biggest change that Beckett "give[s] away" in *Catastrophe* is that which had always made him uncomfortable: his status as the Audience, the dominant force in the auditorium. The dramatist-director-dictator defers to the dissident, to an audience of one in the "dark offstage" of a distant cell that asks nothing and receives everything. As Winnie says, "Someone is looking at me still. [*Pause.*] Caring for me still. [*Pause.*] That is what I find so wonderful" (*Happy Days* 299). Beckett reconciles his paradoxical urge to communicate to an empty house by having a full house interact with a single human being, a dialogue that betrays neither his audience, nor his play, nor himself: a shy man speaking quietly into a void that listens.

* * *

This essay has explored Beckett's troubled relationship with an audience that he largely avoided and whose opinions he invariably rejected. At the heart of his ambivalence resides a solipsistic dependency between watcher and watched that instigated in him an artistic crisis of Pirandellian proportions. For Beckett's plays, like the creatures that inhabit them, need an audience in order to exist; just as Beckett's audience, seeking vainly for recognizable characters, needs his plays in order to spectate. Perhaps as an attempt to reconcile, or at least equilibrate, this ontological servility, Beckett set about manipulating the audience's environment—the auditorium—in relation to his stage, with a diligence that increasingly bordered on domination. The "proscenium" plays force us to recognize through absence, through a kind of cathartic cold turkey, our dependence on Beckett's characters, without whose recognition we become pointless. Players fight for the right to be heard and patrons for the right to hear, both fearing imminent betrayal by the theatrical event itself. Beckett's "elliptical" *dramaticules* increasingly enact this betrayal, sucking life from his creatures, light from the stage, and darkness from the auditorium to fill the void. As the division between stage and auditorium dissolves, the audience—participants by propinquity—approaches annihilation. Yet into this suffocating darkness even the tip of a burning cigar enlightens. By returning light to the stage of *Catastrophe* and allowing it to spill into the auditorium, thereby illuminating the theatrical architecture and reauthorizing the audience, Beckett finally relinquishes control. Switching on the lights, he begins the process of switching off his career.

Notes

1. Vivian Mercier summed up Beckett's ability to confound in the remark that *Godot* is a play in which "nothing happens—twice," while Beckett himself admitted to the "power of [*Endgame*'s] text to claw" (Harmon 11).

2. All citations of Beckett's plays are from *Samuel Beckett: Dramatic Works*, the Grove Centenary Edition, vol. III.

3. In a rehearsal photograph from the Schiller-Theater production of *Endgame* in 1967, Beckett's conversation with Nagg and Nell in their ashbins is conducted at head height, the actors on the stage and Beckett standing below them in the auditorium (Dukes 27).

4. Beckett wrote to Alan Schneider: "Shower (rain). Shower & Cooker are derived from German '*schauen*' & '*kucken*' (to look). They represent the onlooker (audience) wanting to know the meaning of things" (Harmon 95).

5. Friedman's book, *Party Pieces: Oral Storytelling and Social Performance in Joyce and Beckett*, examines the "social performances . . . embedded in the fiction of James Joyce and the drama of Samuel Beckett" (xv).

6. Interview with Peter Woodthorpe, 1994. The passage refers to Beckett's disappointment upon watching a BBC broadcast on 26 April 1960. He concluded, "My play wasn't written for this box. My play was written for small men locked in a big space. Here you're all too big for the place" (Knowlson 435).

7. George Devine, director of the National Theatre production of *Play*, likened the light to a dental drill, an image the actress playing W2, Billie Whitelaw, took a step further: "It is a torturer" (Gontarski xix).

8. Lambert called the figure a "Cro-Magnon man mourning across the aeons," and Harold Hobson wrote, "the dramatic force of the play lies in this strange figure . . . even more than it does in the attention-catching mouth" (Beryl and John Fletcher 210).

9. Beckett telegraphed his response to Jessica Tandy's concern that *Not I*'s running time of twenty-three minutes rendered it incomprehensible: "I am not unduly concerned with intelligibility. I hope the piece may work on the nerves of the audience, not its intellect."

10. Beckett describes W in *Not I*: "I knew that woman's voice in Ireland. . . . There were so many of those old crones, stumbling down the lanes, in the ditches, by the hedgerows" (Knowlson 522).

Works Cited

Beckett, Samuel. *Dramatic Works III.* Ed. Paul Auster. New York: Grove, 2006.

Blau, Henry. *The Audience.* Baltimore: Johns Hopkins UP, 1990.

Cohn, Ruby. *A Beckett Canon.* Ann Arbor: U of Michigan P, 2001.

Duckworth, Colin. *Angels of Darkness: Dramatic Effect in Samuel Beckett with Special Reference to Eugene Ionesco.* London: Allen and Unwin, 1972.

Dukes, Gerry. *Samuel Beckett: Illustrated Lives.* London: Penguin, 2001.

Fletcher, Beryl S., and John Fletcher. *A Student's Guide to the Plays of Samuel Beckett.* London: Faber & Faber, 1978.

Friedman, Alan W. *Party Pieces: Oral Storytelling and Social Performance in Joyce and Beckett.* Syracuse: Syracuse UP, 2007.

Gontarski, S. E., ed. *The Theatrical Notebooks of Samuel Beckett: The Shorter Plays.* New York: Faber & Faber, 1999.

Harmon, Maurice. *No Author Better Served: The Correspondence of Samuel Beckett and Alan Schneider.* Cambridge: Harvard UP, 1998.

Henderson, Cathy, and Dave Oliphant, eds. *Shouting in the Evening: the British Theater.* Austin: Harry Ransom Center, U of Texas at Austin, 1996.

Kalb, Jonathan. *Beckett in Performance.* Cambridge: Cambridge UP, 1989.

Kenner, Hugh. *A Reader's Guide to Samuel Beckett.* Syracuse: Syracuse UP, 1973.

Knowlson, James. *Damned to Fame.* New York: Grove, 1996.

———, ed. *The Theatrical Notebooks of Samuel Beckett.* New York: Grove, 1992.

Knowlson, James, and John Pilling. *Frescoes of the Skull: the Later Prose and Drama of Samuel Beckett.* New York: Grove, 1979.

Levy, Shimon. The Sensitive Chaos: Samuel Beckett's Self-Referential Drama. Brighton: Sussex Academic P, 2002.

Lyons, Charles R. *Samuel Beckett.* New York: Grove, 1983.

Tynan, Kenneth. *A View of the English Stage: 1944–63.* London: Davis-Poytner, 1975.

Chronology

1906	Born April 13 at Foxrock, near Dublin, second son of William and Mary Beckett.
1919–23	Attends Portora Royal School, Enniskillen, an Anglo-Irish boarding school.
1923–27	Attends Trinity College, Dublin; earns bachelor of arts in French and Italian.
1928	Begins two-year fellowship at Ecole Normale Supérieure in Paris. Friendship with Joyce begins, as does immersion in the work of Descartes.
1929	Early writings in *Transition*.
1930	*Whoroscope* wins competition for best poem on the subject of time.
1931	*Proust* published. Returns to Dublin as assistant to professor of romance languages at Trinity. *Le Kid*, parody of Corneille, produced in Dublin.
1933	Death of William Beckett. Begins three-year stay in London.
1934	*More Pricks Than Kicks* published.
1936	Travels in Germany.
1937	Returns to Paris.

1938	Sustains serious stab wound from stranger. Begins relationship with Suzanne Dumesnil. Publishes *Murphy*.
1939	Returns to Paris after Irish sojourn.
1940	Active in French Resistance movement.
1942	Flees to unoccupied France to escape Gestapo. Works as day laborer in farming for two years. Writes *Watt*.
1945	Goes to Ireland after German surrender. Returns to France for service with Irish Red Cross. Returns to Paris permanently.
1946–50	Productive period of writing in French, including the trilogy *Molloy*, *Malone meurt*, and *L'Innommable* and the play *En attendant Godot*.
1947	*Murphy* published in French.
1950	Visits Ireland at the time of his mother's death.
1951	*Molloy* and *Malone meurt* published.
1952	*Godot* published.
1953	First performance of *Godot* in Paris. *Watt* published. *L'Innommable* published.
1955	*Waiting for Godot* opens in London.
1956	*Waiting for Godot* opens in Miami, Florida, for first American performance.
1957	*All That Fall* broadcast by BBC. *Fin de partie* published; first performance (in French) in London.
1958	*Krapp's Last Tape* and *Endgame* (in English) open in London.
1959	*Embers* broadcast by BBC. Honorary degree from Trinity College, Dublin.
1961	*Comment c'est* published. *Happy Days* opens in New York City. Shares, with Borges, International Publisher's Prize.
1962	Marries Suzanne Dumesnil, March 25. *Words and Music* broadcast by the BBC.
1963	*Play* performed at Ulm. *Cascando* broadcast in Paris.
1964	Goes to New York City to help produce his *Film* (with Buster Keaton).

1969	Receives the Nobel Prize in Literature.
1972	*The Lost Ones* published.
1976	*Fizzles* and *All Strange Away* published.
1980	*Company* published.
1989	Dies in Paris on December 22 of respiratory failure.
1990	*As the Story Was Told* published.
1991	*Stirrings Still* published.
1993	*Dream of Fair to Middling Women* and *Nowhow On* published.

Contributors

HAROLD BLOOM is Sterling Professor of the Humanities at Yale University. Educated at Cornell and Yale universities, he is the author of more than 30 books, including *Shelley's Mythmaking* (1959), *The Visionary Company* (1961), *Blake's Apocalypse* (1963), *Yeats* (1970), *The Anxiety of Influence* (1973), *A Map of Misreading* (1975), *Kabbalah and Criticism* (1975), *Agon: Toward a Theory of Revisionism* (1982), *The American Religion* (1992), *The Western Canon* (1994), *Omens of Millennium: The Gnosis of Angels, Dreams, and Resurrection* (1996), *Shakespeare: The Invention of the Human* (1998), *How to Read and Why* (2000), *Genius: A Mosaic of One Hundred Exemplary Creative Minds* (2002), *Hamlet: Poem Unlimited* (2003), *Where Shall Wisdom Be Found?* (2004), and *Jesus and Yahweh: The Names Divine* (2005). In addition, he is the author of hundreds of articles, reviews, and editorial introductions. In 1999, Professor Bloom received the American Academy of Arts and Letters' Gold Medal for Criticism. He has also received the International Prize of Catalonia, the Alfonso Reyes Prize of Mexico, and the Hans Christian Andersen Bicentennial Prize of Denmark.

MARTIN ESSLIN was professor emeritus of drama at Stanford University and also a theater critic. His publications include *The Theatre of the Absurd* (which coined that phrase), *The Anatomy of Drama*, and many other works. He also edited *Twentieth Century Interpretations of Samuel Beckett.*

ALAN S. LOXTERMAN is an emeritus professor in the English department at the University of Richmond. He has published articles as well as interviews with famous poets. He also has contributed to *Finnegans Wake: A Casebook.*

HERSH ZEIFMAN is on the faculty at York University, Toronto. He is the coeditor of *Contemporary British Drama*, a member of the editorial advisory boards of *Modern Drama* and *The Pinter Review*, and former president of the Samuel Beckett Society.

GIUSEPPINA RESTIVO has been a professor at the University of Trieste, Italy, where she has also held administrative duties, including those of deputy dean. She is a published author and a coeditor and also has collaborated with international journals, including *Samuel Beckett Today/Aujourd'hui* and *The Beckett Journal.*

LOIS GORDON is a professor of English at Fairleigh Dickinson University. Some of her recent books include *The World of Samuel Beckett, 1906–1946*; *Pinter at 70*; and *American Chronicle: Year by Year Through the Twentieth Century.*

DECLAN KIBERD is a professor at University College Dublin at Dublin, where he is also chairman of Anglo-Irish literature and drama. Among other titles he has published *The Irish Writer and the World* and *Irish Classics.* He wrote the commentary for the RTÉ television documentary on Beckett, *Silence to Silence.*

ERIC P. LEVY is an associate professor at the University of British Columbia in Vancouver. He is the author of *Beckett and the Voice of Species: A Study of the Prose Fiction* and *Hamlet and the Rethinking of Man.*

ENOCH BRATER is a professor of dramatic literature at the University of Michigan. He has written extensively on Beckett, including the titles *The Essential Samuel Beckett* and *The Drama in the Text: Beckett's Late Fiction.* He is a past president of the Samuel Beckett Society.

MATTHEW DAVIES was a professional actor in the United Kingdom for many years. He continues to act as well as direct in both the academic and professional communities. He is a graduate student at the University of Texas at Austin.

Bibliography

Abbott, H. Porter. *Beckett Writing Beckett: The Author in the Autography*. Ithaca, N.Y.: Cornell University Press, 1996.

Adelman, Gary. *Naming Beckett's Unnamable*. Lewisburg: Bucknell University Press; London: Associated University Presses, 2004.

Alvarez, A. *Beckett*. London: Fontana, 1992.

Barfield, Steven, Philip Tew, and Matthew Feldman, eds. *Beckett and Death*. London; New York: Continuum, 2009.

Begam, Richard. *Samuel Beckett and the End of Modernity*. Stanford, Calif.: Stanford University Press, 1996.

Ben-Zvi, Linda, and Angela Moorjani, ed. *Beckett at 100: Revolving It All*. New York: Oxford University Press, 2008.

Bixby, Patrick. *Samuel Beckett and the Postcolonial Novel*. Cambridge; New York: Cambridge University Press, 2009.

Boulter, Jonathan. *Beckett: A Guide for the Perplexed*. London; New York: Continuum, 2008.

———. *Interpreting Narrative in the Novels of Samuel Beckett*. Gainesville: University Press of Florida, 2001.

Boxall, Peter. *Since Beckett: Contemporary Writing in the Wake of Modernism*. London; New York: Continuum, 2009.

Calder, John. *The Philosophy of Samuel Beckett*. London: Calder, 2001.

Casanova, Samuel. *Beckett: Anatomy of a Literary Revolution*, translated by Gregory Elliott. London; New York: Verso, 2006.

Davies, Paul. *The Ideal Real: Beckett's Fiction and Imagination*. Rutherford: Fairleigh Dickinson University Press; London; Cranbury, N.J.: Associated University Presses, 1994.

Dowd, Garin. *Abstract Machines: Samuel Beckett and Philosophy after Deleuze and Guattari*. Amsterdam: Rodopi, 2007.

Drew, Anne Marie, ed. *Past Crimson, Past Woe: The Shakespeare-Beckett Connection*. New York: Garland, 1993.

Essif, Les. *Empty Figure on an Empty Stage: The Theatre of Samuel Beckett and His Generation*. Bloomington: Indiana University Press, 2001.

Feldman, Matthew. *Beckett's Books: A Cultural History of Samuel Beckett's "Interwar Notes."* New York; London: Continuum, 2006.

Fletcher, John. *About Beckett: The Playwright and the Work*. London; New York: Faber and Faber, 2003.

Gendron, Sarah. *Repetition, Difference, and Knowledge in the Work of Samuel Beckett, Jacques Derrida, and Gilles Deleuze*. New York: Peter Lang, 2008.

Gontarski, S. E., and Anthony Uhlmann, ed. *Beckett after Beckett*. Gainesville: University Press of Florida, 2006.

Gussow, Mel. *Conversations with (and about) Beckett*. London: Nick Hern Books, 1996.

Jeffers, Jennifer M. *Beckett's Masculinity*. New York: Palgrave Macmillan, 2009.

Jeffers, Jennifer M., ed. *Samuel Beckett: A Casebook*. New York; London: Garland, 1998.

Karic, Pol Popovic. *Ironic Samuel Beckett: Samuel Beckett's Life and Drama:* Waiting for Godot, Endgame, *and* Happy Days. Lanham, Md.: University Press of America, 2007.

Katz, Daniel. *Saying I No More: Subjectivity and Consciousness in the Prose of Samuel Beckett*. Evanston, Ill.: Northwestern University Press, 1999.

Keller, John Robert. *Samuel Beckett and the Primacy of Love*. Manchester; New York: Manchester University Press, 2002.

Kim, Hwa Soon. *The Counterpoint of Hope, Obsession, and Desire for Death in Five Plays by Samuel Beckett*. New York: Peter Lang, 1996.

Locatelli, Carla. *Unwording the World: Samuel Beckett's Prose Works after the Nobel Prize*. Philadelphia: University of Pennsylvania Press, 1990.

Maude, Ulrika, and Matthew Feldman, ed. *Beckett and Phenomenology*. London; New York: Continuum, 2009.

McMullan, Anna, and S. E. Wilmer, ed. *Reflections on Beckett: A Centenary Celebration*. Ann Arbor: University of Michigan Press, 2009.

Morin, Emilie. *Samuel Beckett and the Problem of Irishness*. Basingstoke [England]; New York: Palgrave Macmillan, 2009.

Murphy, P. J. *Beckett's Dedalus: Dialogical Engagements with Joyce in Beckett's Fiction*. Toronto: University of Toronto Press, 2009.

Pultar, Gönül. *Technique and Tradition in Beckett's Trilogy of Novels*. Lanham, Md.: University Press of America, 1996.

Rabinovitz, Rubin. *Innovation in Samuel Beckett's Fiction*. Urbana: University of Illinois Press, 1992.

Smith, Joseph, ed. *The World of Samuel Beckett*. Baltimore: Johns Hopkins University Press, 1991.

Smith, Russell, ed. *Beckett and Ethics*. London: Continuum, 2008.

Stewart, Bruce, ed. *Beckett and Beyond*. Gerrards Cross, Buckinghamshire, UK: Colin Smythe, 1999.

Stewart, Paul. *Zone of Evaporation: Samuel Beckett's Disjunctions*. Amsterdam; New York: Rodopi, 2006.

Szafraniec, Asja. *Beckett, Derrida, and the Event of Literature*. Stanford, Calif.: Stanford University Press, 2007.

Trezise, Thomas. *Into the Breach: Samuel Beckett and the Ends of Literature*. Princeton, N.J.: Princeton University Press, 1990.

Uhlmann, Anthony. *Samuel Beckett and the Philosophical Image*. Cambridge, UK; New York: Cambridge University Press, 2006.

Watt, Stephen. *Beckett and Contemporary Irish Writing*. Cambridge; New York: Cambridge University Press, 2009.

Weisberg, David. *Chronicles of Disorder: Samuel Beckett and the Cultural Politics of the Modern Novel*. Albany: State University of New York Press, 2000.

Weller, Shane. *A Taste for the Negative: Beckett and Nihilism*. London: Legenda, 2005.

White, Kathryn. *Beckett and Decay*. London; New York: Continuum, 2009.

Worth, Katharine. *Samuel Beckett's Theatre: Life Journeys*. Oxford; New York: Clarendon Press, 1999.

Wynands, Sandra. *Iconic Spaces: The Dark Theology of Samuel Beckett's Drama*. Notre Dame, Ind.: University of Notre Dame Press, 2007.

Acknowledgments

Martin Esslin, "Telling It How It Is: Beckett and the Mass Media." From *The World of Samuel Beckett*, edited by Joseph H. Smith, pp 204–16. Published by the Johns Hopkins University Press. Copyright © 1991 by the Forum on Psychiatry and the Humanities of the Washington School of Psychiatry.

Alan S. Loxterman, "'The More Joyce Knew the More He Could' and 'More Than I Could': Theology and Fictional Technique in Joyce and Beckett." From *Re: Joyce'n Beckett*, edited by Phyllis Carey and Ed Jewinski, pp. 61–82. Copyright © 1992 by Fordham University.

Hersh Zeifman, "The Syntax of Closure: Beckett's Late Drama." From *Beckett On and On . . .*, edited by Lois Oppenheim and Marius Buning, pp 240–54. Published by Fairleigh Dickinson University Press. Copyright © 1996 by Associated University Presses.

Giuseppina Restivo, "Caliban/Clov and Leopardi's Boy: Beckett and Postmodernism." From *Beckett and Beyond*, edited by Bruce Stewart, pp. 217–30. Copyright © 1999 by the Princess Grace Irish Library, Monaco.

Lois Gordon, "The Language of Dreams: The Anatomy of the Conglomerative Effect." From *Reading Godot*, pp. 97–11, 189–92. Copyright © 2002 by Yale University. Reprinted with permission.

Declan Kiberd, "Murphy and the World of Samuel Beckett." From *Samuel Beckett— 100 Years: Centenary Essays*, edited by Christopher Murray, pp. 34–47. Copyright © 2006 by RTÉ.

Eric P. Levy, "Disintegrative Process in *Endgame*." From *Trapped in Thought: A Study of the Beckettian Mentality*, pp. 162–79. Copyright © 2007 by Syracuse University Press.

Enoch Brater, "Beckett's 'Beckett': So Many Words for Silence." From *Reflections on Beckett: A Centenary Celebration*, edited by Anna McMullan and S. E. Wilmer, pp. 190–203. Copyright © 2009 by the University of Michigan.

Matthew Davies, "'Someone is looking at me still': The Audience–Creature Relationship in the Theater Plays of Samuel Beckett." From *Texas Studies in Literature and Language* 51, no. 1 (Spring 2009): 76–93. Copyright © 2009 by the University of Texas Press.

Index

Characters in literary works are indexed by first name (if any), followed by the name of the work in parentheses